I0482884

Forex Strategies Revealed

By Ade Asefeso MCIPS MBA

Copyright 2014 by Ade Asefeso MCIPS MBA
All rights reserved.

Second Edition

ISBN-13: 978-1499680003

ISBN-10: 1499680007

Publisher: AA Global Sourcing Ltd
Website: http://www.aaglobalsourcing.com

1

Table of Contents

Disclaimer..7

Dedication...8

Chapter 1: Introduction to Forex Trading..............9

Chapter 2: Forex (Foreign Exchange Market)
Scams...13

Chapter 3: Forex Trading be Afraid, be Very Afraid
....15

Chapter 4: The Importance of Forex Trading
Education...19

Chapter 5: Textbook Mistakes in Forex Trading..23

Chapter 6: Forex Trading Courses Online..............27

Chapter 7: Effective Advices for Forex Trading
Beginners...29

Chapter 8: There's Money to be had in Forex
Trading, But it's Risky for a First-time Investor ...33

Chapter 9: Why get into Forex Trading.................37

Chapter 10: Learning the Ropes of Forex Trading
and Getting Ahead of the Game Early On............41

Chapter 11: Essential Tips on how to Learn Forex
Trading...45

Chapter 12: New Forms of Income Generating
Businesses from the Internet: Becoming a Forex
Trader...49

Chapter 13: The Importance of a Good Investment
Program on Forex Trading.......................................53

Chapter 14: A Forex Demo shows you how it Works before you Jump into it for Real................57

Chapter 15: Simulated Forex Trading uses Simulators as Trader's Guides..................................59

Chapter 16: Practicing in the Forex Market...........63

Chapter 17: Mini Forex Trading: Lesser Stakes, Greater Possibilities......................................65

Chapter 18: Should you Try Forex Arbitrage........69

Chapter 19: Forex Research for Success on the Market..71

Chapter 20: What is Online Forex Trading Broker System? the Question Each Forex Green Horn Should Ask..73

Chapter 21: The Forex Market uses Margins to Increase your Profits...................................77

Chapter 22: The Basics of Reading a Forex Quote 79

Chapter 23: Trying to Forecast Forex Rates is an Acquired Skill...81

Chapter 24: Online Forex Forums Connect Traders Around the World.................................83

Chapter 25: Forex Trading, what the Hype is all About...85

Chapter 26: The Internet and Forex Trading: the Perfect Combination 87

Chapter 27: The Different Options you can Avail to Learn Forex Trading.............................91

Chapter 28: Tips on Managing Islamic Forex Trading Accounts...95

Chapter 29: When it Comes to Smart Investing, all World News is Forex News. 99

Chapter 30: What are Forex Robots? 101

Chapter 31: Newbies Forex Robots.....................105

Chapter 32: Forex Robot Myths..........................109

Chapter 33: Its More than one kind of Forex Robots 113

Chapter 34: The Secret Behind Forex Robots 117

Chapter 35: Creating Profitable Forex Trading Systems in Five Easy Steps.............................121

Chapter 36: Types of Automated Forex Trading System...125

Chapter 37: Tips when Choosing the Right Forex Robot..129

Chapter 38: Forex Robot Advantages 133

Chapter 39: The Risks of a Forex Robot.............137

Chapter 40: Let your Money Work for you with Automated Forex Trading.................................141

Chapter 41: Do you Need to Buy a Forex System? 143

Chapter 42: Forge your Forex Trading-Strategy .145

Chapter 43: Is Forex Scalping for You? 149

Chapter 44: Forex Alerts are a Handy Way of Staying on Top of the Market...........................153

Chapter 45: Using the Forex Trade Signal to your Advantage 155

Chapter 46: How to Read a Forex Chart............157

Chapter 47: Forex Trading Online......................159

5

Chapter 48: How to Succeed in Online Forex Day Trading 163

Chapter 49: Forex Technical Indicators Revealed 167

Chapter 50: Forex Trading Signals: Indicators of a Better Timing Trade 173

Chapter 51: Using Forex Signals to Navigate the Currency Market 177

Chapter 52: Factors that Influence Forex Market Trends 181

Chapter 53: Hedging Your Bets Against the Future 185

Chapter 54: Forex Trading: Information that you should Always Watch out For 189

Chapter 55: Stock Trading and Forex 193

Chapter 56: The Advantages of Forex Trading in the Stock Markets 197

Chapter 57: Forex Trading: What to Trade, When to Trade, and how to Trade 201

Chapter 58: Forex Trading: How to be Successful 207

Chapter 59: Forex Brokers: Assisting you with your Trading Needs 213

Chapter 60: Finding a Forex Broker in a Crowded Marketplace 217

Chapter 61: How to Find Available Forex Jobs .221

Chapter 62: Conclusion 223

Disclaimer

This publication is designed to provide competent and reliable information regarding the subject matter covered. However, it is sold with the understanding that the author and publisher are not engaged in rendering professional advice. The authors and publishers specifically disclaim any liability that is incurred from the use or application of contents of this book.

If you purchased this book without a cover you should be aware that this book may have been stolen property and reported as "unsold and destroyed" to the publisher. In this case neither the author nor the publisher has received any payment for this "stripped book."

Dedication

To my family and friends who seems to have been sent here to teach me something about who I am supposed to be. They have nurtured me, challenged me, and even opposed me.... But at every juncture has taught me!

This book is dedicated to my lovely boys, Thomas, Michael and Karl. Teaching them to manage their finance will give them the lives they deserve. They have taught me more about life, presence, and energy management than anything I have done in my life.

Chapter 1: Introduction to Forex Trading

The foreign exchange, or forex, market is relatively young, having begun in the early 1970s after the United States dropped the gold standard and national currencies started to fluctuate widely. For about 30 years prior to that, most nations had agreed to keep their currency values stable in relation to the U.S. dollar, making a forex market unnecessary. With that no longer the case, banks quickly realized that a profit could be made in "buying" currency when it was devalued and 'selling" it after it strengthened, just like any other commodity.

If you are just starting out in the stock trading business or if you are already in it, you may have heard the term Forex trading quite a few times, but you probably might not have a clue on what it may actually mean.

Forex or foreign exchange trading is actually the largest and a fast-rising financial industry in stock trading these days. Here is a quick introduction to trading in foreign exchange.

What is Forex Trading?

The Foreign Exchange market (Forex) is actually the largest financial market in the world. It actually makes a volume of over 2 trillion U.S. dollars a day, and as compared to its counterpart –the New York Stock

Exchange (NYSE) which usually only trades a volume of 25 billion dollars each day, this industry is so huge that it becomes a profitable playground for many investors including central banks, large banks, multinational companies and even governments.

What is actually traded on the foreign exchange is money. It actually consists of the concurrent buying and selling of currencies, which are traded through brokers and are traded in pairs.

When you are buying currency, it is like you are investing on the economy of a particular country. For example, if you buy U.S. dollars then it is as if you are buying a share of the U.S. economy. Whatever the market thinks about the current health of a country's economy would directly be reflected on the price of its legal tender and this is how currencies go up or down.

Forex Trading For The Masses

Originally the whole concept of trading in the Foreign Exchange was only intended for huge companies and banks, but not for normal citizens. After all, you could only take part in the trade if you have around ten to fifty million dollars minimum.

However, with the rise of globalization through the Internet, trading is now offered to retail traders. And these days, almost anyone can now invest on the foreign trade. All you really need to join is some small amount of money, a computer and a high-speed Internet connection, and you can sign up for an account with online Forex trading firms.

There is no exact physical office for Foreign Exchange unlike its counterpart in New York. However, the three main centres for this trade are United States, United Kingdom and Japan. These countries handle majority of Forex transactions and trades goes on for 24 hours everyday.

Today, the Foreign Exchange, as the largest market in the world, is fast paced and enormous. And it has become a very lucrative arena for many traders who may have had participated in stock trading and in other markets. Many large institutions and even smaller-based individuals have gone out to play in this market.

Although this particular market gives huge promises, remember that there is still too much at stake. It is estimated that around 70 to 90 percent of the Foreign Exchange market is still speculative. And the parties that trade currencies may not always have a plan to actually take delivery of the said currency, and more are still speculating on movement of money.

If you are interested in investing in this particular arena, take time to be familiar with the game and make sure you get the right educational background. Taking the extra mile will all be worth it, and once you have tasted your success in this arena, you will be ready to take on anything in trading.

Chapter 2: Forex (Foreign Exchange Market) Scams

The foreign exchange market is also known as FX or it is also found to be referred to as the FOREX. All three of these have the same meaning, which is the trade of trading between different companies, banks, businesses, and governments that are located in different countries. The financial market is one that is always changing leaving transactions required to be completed through brokers, and banks. Many scams have been emerging in the FOREX business, as foreign companies and people are setting up online to take advantage of people who do not realize that foreign trade must take place through a broker or a company with direct participation involved in foreign exchanges.

Cash, stocks, and currency are traded through the foreign exchange markets. The FOREX market will be present and exist when one currency is traded for another. Think about a trip you may take to a foreign country. Where are you going to be able to 'trade your money' for the value of the money that is in that other country? This is FOREX trading basis, and it is not available in all banks, and it is not available in all financial centres. FOREX is a specialized trading circumstance. Small business and individuals often times looking to make big money, are the victims of scams when it comes to learning about FOREX and the foreign trade markets. As FOREX is seen as how to make a quick buck or two, people don't question their participation in such an event, but if you are not investing money through a broker in the FOREX market, you could easily end up losing everything that you have invested in the transaction.

Scams to be wary of A FOREX scam is one that involves trading but will turn out to be a fraud; you have no chance of getting your money back once you have invested it. If you were to invest money with a company stating they are involved in FOREX trading you want read closely to learn if they are permitted to do business in your country. Many companies are not permitted in the FOREX market, as they have defrauded investors before.

In the last five years, with the help of the Internet, FOREX trading and the awareness of FOREX trading has become all the rage. Banks are the number one source for FOREX trading to take place, where a trained and licensed broker is going to complete transactions and requirements you set forth. Commissions are paid on the transaction and this is the usual.

Another type of scam that is prevalent in the FOREX markets is software that will aid you in making trades, in learning about the foreign markets and in practicing so you can prepare yourself for following and making trades. You want to be able to rely on a program or software that is really going to make a difference. Consult with your financial broker or your bank to learn more about FOREX trading, the FX markets and how you can avoid being the victim while investing in these markets.

Chapter 3: Forex Trading be Afraid, be Very Afraid

A lot of individuals are interested to know more about FOREX trading. Do you want to know why? Well, Forex trading can help you earn lots of money as long as you have the right strategies and trading information. However, with one false move, you can also lose huge money. To be a successful trader, you need to be serious with all your trading transactions.

Exchanges in the Forex market happen instantaneously. Even the expert traders and bankers are challenged to make very good and well-informed trades. A single Forex trade should be done after carefully considering some factors.

Before, only the world's largest banks were allowed to trade openly. Things have changed greatly since the introduction of the internet. If you have an internet connection, you can already join in Forex trading. Many people are now actively involved in Forex trading because the market is very liquid.

According to the expert traders, it is easy to trade in the Forex market but for the newbies, it may be a bit difficult. You see, there are some things that you need to consider.

Many traders lose their capital and according to statistics, these traders make up 90% of the total number of traders in the Forex market. The other

10% is still split into two wherein the 5% are the breakeven traders and other 5% are those traders that attain beneficial results. The percentage of successful Forex traders is indeed very small as compared to the unsuccessful ones; because of this fact, many individuals are scared to invest in the Forex market.

If you want to make huge profits, one way to do that is to join Forex trading. However, to consistently earn money, you have to improve the odds involved in trading.

Education is vital if you want to succeed as a Forex trader. You should have adequate knowledge about the market and every detail you can learn is very important. You can also learn many things in Forex trading. In fact, in every transaction you make, you are bound to learn something that you can use in your future exchanges.

As a Forex trader, you should have your very own strategy or trading system. Many individuals find it difficult to follow rules and guidelines and if you are like that, the Forex market is not the place for you. You must be very strict in following your devised strategies or trading system. This is the only way to earn more profits.

Aside from having your own trading system and strategies, you should be able to analyze and study the price behaviour in the Forex market. Prices tend to change rather quickly and so you need to be prepared at all times. Surprises in the Forex market are natural and you should be prepared for them.

The buying or selling decisions of traders are often influenced by psychological issues. Not all traders are rationally thinking in every transaction they make and you can use this knowledge to your advantage. That way, you can easily decide when to enter or exit.

Successful traders know how to manage their money or investment. You have to ensure that the trading account is adequately funded and you should not enter into any transaction blindly.

Now that you know something about Forex trading, don't you think it's time that you also trade in the market? If you are willing to take some risks, you can surely earn huge profits.

Chapter 4: The Importance of Forex Trading Education

Many Americans, British or even other foreign nationalities are interested in getting involved on Forex trading. Who on Earth will decline to the wealth offered by the Forex market, which is the largest market around the world; a whooping $2 trillion U.S. dollars worth of daily turnovers. Anyone inside the Forex clan has the opportunity of getting a big slice of that huge wealth. Aside from the huge possibilities for its traders, Forex market provides an extensive list of benefits, round the clock financial transactions, extreme liquidity, real-time and efficient trade executions and the list goes on.

However, before taking home the "bacon", you need to get a Forex trading education. Just like any other investments, you should never step on the Forex ground without knowing what you are stepping into. With proper education regarding Forex trading, you are assured that you are on the right track and you are on your way in making substantial profit.

If you want to succeed in any endeavour, you need to have persistence and dedication. Even your daily life requires it because if you are the type of person who is quite lazy and wants to goof around, you will attain nothing of importance in your life.

Ever since you were a little kid, you were already taught with the value of good education. From your nursery days, until you finally graduate in University or college, you have dedicated many years to get a good education. But it doesn't end there.

Each time you encounter a new endeavour, activity, or thing, the first to come into your mind is to learn about that particular thing or activity. So you see, no matter what we do, education continues. And this is especially true with forex trading.

Statistics have shown that over 94% professional traders lose a lot of money every day in forex trading alone. But do not be discouraged; in fact why not use that piece of information to strive hard to get a forex trading education.

The financial market changes by the minute, or even by the second. Who knows which currencies are a good buy and which are not. Most traders, specially the starters, believe that they can predict what is about to happen in forex trading. But you see there is more to predicting the market; you need to educate yourself still.

First things first, you must have a forex trading system which contains the key elements, namely: money management, risk, and execution. If you have a well developed system, which gives a lot of weight to money and risk management, over time you can actually carry on draw downs while expecting consistent returns.

Forex trading is not just about buying low currencies and then selling them when the price is high. Profitable traders can teach you more than just discipline, because you also need to learn about detachment. Ask a professional trader to show and guide you how it is done.

You must have the proper mindset in order to be a successful forex trader. To achieve this, your capital should have a positive return. It is not all about profits especially when you are just a beginner. You should first determine if you have a reasonable return of your capital.

Most successful forex traders have undergone some sort of education. Since forex trading is a high risk endeavour, it is not wise to instantly jump into the trade.

If you purely rely on experience and instinct, you may not likely succeed in forex trading. But if you have undergone a forex trading education, you are more capable to handle demands and the stress that comes along with the trade.

Through forex education, you can learn all about the market mechanics, reading the forex chart, how software works, how it is closed, the right time to bid, and many more. It is the best possible route to take before plunging into forex trading.

The FX market is volatile, and you can understand the situation better if you know how to read charts. It will be easier for you to understand the different reasons behind these shifts, and can greatly help in minimizing the risks that you are going to undertake.

The very first things that you will learn in forex trading education are the basics. It includes margin concepts, order types, rollovers, bids, and leveraging. Aside from that, you can also learn about fundamental and technical analysis. And lastly, you should learn about trading psychology which can teach you about patience, discipline, and commitment.

It is also good if you can learn about the financial market's history. And knowing the past mistakes made by other traders will teach us how to avoid such circumstances. You can get a forex education online or in a traditional class.

Having a forex education is an added advantage compared to those who haven't had any. This is especially helpful for starters, and even for those who have been in trading for some time.

Most professional traders highly recommend some form of forex education. With a little background and knowledge about the trade, it is a sure fire way to succeed in this line of trade. Instead of making wild guesses, why not take a forex education class, and make educated decisions when doing the actual trade.

Chapter 5: Textbook Mistakes in Forex Trading

Novice and students of forex trading often overlook the obvious: many before them have made fatal mistakes. Making the same wrong decisions all over again just does not make sense. What a serious forex trader should do is to learn from them and up their game.

Relearning these assumptions and wrong steps will increase one's chances of succeeding in the business. If you are inexperienced, then the experience of others can only enrich you. Always remember not to make these mistakes:

Wrong timing of Stops:

While stops are certainly essential in forex trading, the wrong timing can topple your whole strategy. Sure, you might be thinking of putting a cork in your money leak, but the key to doing that is the right timing. The trade should still be leaning in your favour. Proper money management should be at play here. Risk should be at the minimum before placing a trade. Calculate and research your options.

Underestimating the risks of leverages:

Okay, you might be thinking of instant profit if you use a 300:1 leverage on a trade. However, are you sure profit will come in? A lot of people think of leverages as free poker chips where in fact, the risks are higher. It is all about making sure you have a good solid hand. Even then, experienced traders are always careful only risk 2-3% of their investment balance on a trade. Asses your risks and gains, do not be dazzled with the money and the excitement.

Relying on signals and indicators too much:

It is as if you are just a sheep following a trend. Signals and indicators are just that: assistants and cues that help you make a decision. Remember that your strategy and assets are unique to you, so technical indicators do not always apply to you. You still need to work. There is no magical formula or machine that can do the work for you.

Day trading:

Some people might think that day trading holds no or fewer risks, which may be true to some. However, there is a reason why long term trading still holds: it gives you more time to wait out a position that will be in your favour, yielding more profits. Day trading can work, but only to a select few.

Getting sucked in by "miracle" software:

There are dozens of so-called powerful platforms and software that tells you can beat the system and reap huge profits. Some of them can help but a lot of them are duds. The main thing to remember is that there is no sole software out there that is foolproof. It's okay to get indicators and advice from a few, but it all rests in your acumen. Before putting your money where your program's mouth is, you better test it thoroughly.

The same thing goes for systems and strategy on paper. Even if you have back tested it, would the conditions you have used to test that be the same conditions that will happen in the near future?

Getting overwhelmed with emotions:

Forex trading requires objectivity, cool thinking and the ability to make sound decisions. Be too afraid to risk, and you will not profit at all. Be too reckless and you will lose your shirt in no time. Here is a smart thing to do; read up on forex trading psychology. Watch yourself and do not work obsessively. Have a life.

There is a reason why forex trading is so popular yet only a select few have built their careers over it. A lot of beginners have failed, but where they have fallen, you should pick up and do better.

Chapter 6: Forex Trading Courses Online

Many years ago, Forex trading was possible when you are in the actual trading platform. If you are not present there, you cannot make a trade. Thanks to the introduction of the internet, it is now possible to conduct the Forex transactions from the comfort of your own home or even in the office. There are now Forex trading courses offered online which can help you with your trading concerns.

The communication industry has definitely contributed a lot to the growth of the Forex market. Trades can be done by way of phone or through online resources. Because of this, the Forex market is far larger than other major financial markets. By taking up trading courses on the internet, you can learn a lot about Forex trading. Newbies in the industry will definitely learn a great deal about this market and how to conduct their trades. A lot of things are free online but the trading courses require a minimal fee. The knowledge that you can gain from these courses are nothing compared to the fee that you are going to pay. Besides, if you can become a good trader, you can earn more profits.

Before signing up for a trading course, you need to consider things like:

1. Who offered the trading course? Was offered by a reputable company or firm?

2. What is the reason behind the course offer?

3. Is the company or firm trying to promote a trading site where you can join in the future?

4. Is the course trying to push you in using a certain trading website? Are you being pushed to invest money?

Answer the questions and from your answers, you can already determine if the trading course is worthy or not.

You have to find a trading course which provides high standard learning.

A good trading course should be able to provide you with different kinds of views from different established companies. It should not concentrate mainly on how a certain company conducts its trade. Look for reputable companies and firms that offer excellent trading courses. With a bit of research online, you will surely find the course that you are looking for. Since you are going to pay for the trading course, it should teach you everything you need to know about Forex trading which includes developing a trading system, using trend indicators, signal generators, flow charts, and many other things. The course should also teach you about the best trading software programs available in the market today.

Start looking for the best trading course online. With a very minimal fee, you can already gain priceless knowledge that you can use when you finally decide to enter the Forex market. Now, Forex trading will not be very difficult for you.

Chapter 7: Effective Advices for Forex Trading Beginners

Not all people are familiar with forex trading. In fact, most people think that when you talk about forex trading, it has something to do with stocks or bonds. But forex trading is different from stocks or bonds. It involves the trading of currency pairs. Currencies are traded in pairs, and you cannot find a particular currency without a pair. The major currencies being traded are chosen above the rest because they are stable and have a greater value than other foreign currencies.

Every time a new comer arrives in the market, the very first ones to take notice of them are what you call frauds. That is why, if you are new in forex trading, you need to take some advice. It does not hurt to ask for advice from the ones who are already engaged in forex trading. In fact, you can make use of their advice for your own good, and even to your advantage.

Since forex trading is globally available, it is not surprising if there are frauds that are able to infiltrate the financial market. To safeguard people from these frauds, they must be made aware of these growing fact, so that they will be able to protect their trading career.

The opportunities that forex trading provides for different individuals, firms, and organizations is growing rapidly every year. And accompanying this growth is the widespread growth of different scams related with forex trading. But you should not worry because there are a lot of legitimate companies or firms that can help you in forex trading.

The best thing to do is to find these legitimate companies to stay away from fraudulent ones. However, most new traders fall prey to these scammers because of their savoury offers.

A piece of advice: stay away from companies or firms which advertise high profits for minimal risks. In today's financial market, if you want to earn high profits, then you are likely subjected to high risks as well. These things always go together.

Always stay on the safe side. If you are looking for a forex trading broker, and of course, each broker is part of a certain company, make sure that you select a government registered company. In signing any contract with them, double check if they are registered or certified brokers. This is a good step to undertake in order to prevent any misfortune that you might encounter in the future.

The job of reducing the risk is entirely yours, not that of the broker; so if the company offers or promises little risks, guaranteed profits, and the like, that is a sure sign that they are there to make a fool out of you.

Professional trader or not, a little use of the common sense can go a long way.

Before doing any forex trade, do your homework. Research all the necessary details about trading. Ever heard of inter-bank market? Stay away from companies which lure you into trading in the inter-bank market because the currency transactions are negotiated in a wobbly network of large companies and financial institutions.

If a certain company does not disclose any information about their background, that should serve as a red flag. It means that you should not continue doing transactions with them. Nor is it advisable to transfer/send cash through the mail or the internet. Practice caution in everything you do, and you will be more than sure that you are always safe.

Fraudulent companies often solicit services and advertise soaring pressure tactics to attract you in participating or joining their services. Offshore companies which guarantee no risk and return of profit are a big no. Always be sceptical and don't jump in to any instant offer that comes your way.

You can decide for yourself. After all these pieces of advice, it will still depend entirely on you whether you will apply it or not. You are the one who will be subject to fraudulent individuals or companies. If you want to protect your forex trading career, carefully consider these things. With patience and a little diligence, you can expect for a successful forex trading career. These frauds which abound in the financial market will not succeed if only people are alert and sceptical.

Chapter 8: There's Money to be had in Forex Trading, But it's Risky for a First-time Investor

Forex trading is done on a much greater scale than any other kind of market in the world. Some 1.9 trillion dollars are handled every single day. About 73 percent of all forex trading is done by 10 international banks with names you're familiar with: Merrill Lynch, Citigroup, and so forth. National banks and other financial institutions account for another chunk of forex trading, and transactions by 'day traders", regular individuals, and people like you and me account for only 2 percent of all trading.

Nonetheless, many average investors do try their hand at forex trading, and there are many financial institutions who handle such transactions. It is known as "retail forex," and it is handled much the same way that day trading of stocks is handled.

The downside is that unlike the stock market, the forex market is not particularly well regulated, and people inexperienced with it can be taken advantage of. The U.S. Commodity Futures Trading Commission (CFTC) gives several bits of advice for amateur forex traders. Among the CFTC's tips:

1. Avoid companies that predict or guarantee large profits, or that promise little or no financial risk. There is ALWAYS a financial risk in forex trading, and no one can guarantee profits when it comes to speculative

endeavours.

2. If someone won't give you his background, don't deal with him. Likewise, always check out a company's track record before doing any trading with them.
3. The Internet is a haven for shady types. Be wary of anyone wanting you to send cash.
4. Above all, remember that if an opportunity sounds too good to be true, it probably is!

There are plenty of honest and reliable forex trading firms out there, including ones that operate online. But even if the trading company is legitimate, there are still risks inherent in trading. Because currency rates can fluctuate for such a variety of reasons, it is difficult to predict what investments to make. Even seasoned professionals get blindsided sometimes.

For example, let's say the market reports this: GBP/EUR 1.2200. That means the cost of buying one British pound is 1.22 euros. If you believed that course was going to change, and the euro was going to become more valuable than the pound, you might sell 100,000 pounds, buy 100,000 euros, and wait. Then let's say a few weeks later, the exchange rate fluctuates to this: EUR/GBP 1.3100. Sure enough, the euro is now worth 1.31 pounds, a profit of 0.11 per unit or it could go the other way.

The forex market is vast and daunting and mostly inhabited by giant organizations. But it can be navigated by individuals who have studied the finer points and who want to take a risk on something potential profitable. And since the whole world uses money, the trading of that money is always going to be a major force in the financial world.

In short, forex trading can be lucrative, but only if you know what you are doing. Before embarking on any investing, study the details of how the market works, what causes fluctuations, how to interpret financial indicators, and all the other ins and outs of the market. Forex trading is not something to be entered into lightly. There is much potential for profit, but there is even greater potential for loss, both at the hands of unscrupulous trading firms, and of your own inexperience.

Chapter 9: Why get into Forex Trading

Why Get into Forex Trading?

There is the stock market and there is the foreign exchange market. The latter is considered the bigger opportunity if you know how it works and if you have the money to invest. There are a lot of reasons nowadays why people are flocking to learn the in and outs of forex trading.

But why get into forex trading anyway? Are there any truths behind the big profit boon we all keep hearing about? These points are the prime reasons why the forex market is so huge right now.

Boundless Activity

The foreign exchange market is open 24 hours on weekdays. Compared to other markets that operate at specific hours and days, the forex market is a buzz of activity and opportunities in the week. Investors can react to specific changes and trends that happen within the week, anytime.

Freedom

This also means freedom from normal office hours; traders can operate whatever time they wish. Naturally, this attracts people from different lifestyles, locales and classes. If you have a laptop, then you can trade no matter where you are.

Less Cost

Add the purely liquid nature of the market and the electronic way of transacting in it then you would have a feature that will definitely attract people: the lesser trading costs. We can do away with the traditional costs that add up to your bill and concentrate on only the spreads. The spreads here are usually smaller than the spreads in other markets, and that would mean better profits.

Leverage

Unlike other markets where leverages are small, forex trading allows for bigger leverages, giving you the chances to trade up to a hundred times your investment. Brokers have features where they can give you a lot of leverage depending on the account. Of course, this also means a bigger risk of losing money. Risk management protects you from this.

Stable Price

Since your trade is done immediately, chances are the prices you saw are what you are going to get. Compared this to other markets, where your transaction often ends in a span of a day or two thus giving a chance for the price to slip and change. The stability and speed attracts a lot of traders in this market. Your assets are not tied up for long periods, giving you more control.

Transparency

Being electronic in transactions and having liquid, movable assets is easier to analyze and manage. Everything can be accessed by your platform and laptop. Your deals can be executed as per your viewpoint and strategy. This gives you a better feel of the market cycle, making your predictions more accurate each time you trade.

Stable Profit Chances

Since your trading involves two currencies and not other markets and trends, one always has the opportunity for profit. There is no bulldog watching of rising or falling of markets, goods and industries. Whether the market is bullish or bearish does not really need to worry you. What really matters is that you pick the right currency to trade.

Forex trading is considered the perfect competition for logical reasons. Everybody is presented with an equal playing field. Even if the currency is falling, it just means that there is currency raising somewhere and the opportunity of profit exists. An unlimited earning potential, the freedom, and the even opportunity makes the foreign exchange market an exciting opportunity for anyone.

Chapter 10: Learning the Ropes of Forex Trading and Getting Ahead of the Game Early On

In the world of cut-throat business, it pays to know your way around. And in the world of forex trading it pays to know the market, the players and the stakes. In forex trading, you need to know what you are looking at, the value of the currency you are trading, the factors that affect the value of your currency, the trading strategies and the market trends.

Fundamental to forex trading is research. But as we are talking about big bucks here, a good forex trading course would be helpful.

Why Go for a Trading Course

A Forex trading course teaches you how to predict or chart the movements of the market as well as the perfect time to buy and sell a commodity. It familiarizes you with the basic terminologies and the process of trading.

Because forex trading is done in real time and decisions are done on the spot, a trader should be emotionally equipped and prepared to handle the demands, challenges and the stress of the market. And these, one can learn in a forex trading education.

What To Look For in Forex Trading Courses

The Basics: A god forex trading education should include in its program the basics on margins, types of orders and leveraging as these are essential in the forex market transactions. It should teach the basic terminologies, the types of analyses being used, the software and tools and other such important things as charting and leverage. These are essential as the trader learns when to cut back and minimize his losses as well as gain profit.

Analysis: It should also teach you how to analyze common mistakes and at the same time, the ways to avoid such mistakes. Basic to a forex trading course is a detailed discussion on doing technical and fundamental analysis and tools.

Values: More than the theories and the basics involved, a good forex trading education should teach you proper money management and the development of a proper trading disposition and psychology. As the stakes are upped, a trader may become too emotionally involved. It is important that a forex trading course develops the appropriate values needed in money trading, such as discipline, patience and commitment.

Experience: A good forex trading course should provide real life experience through apprenticeship. There is no better teacher than experience, they say, and as forex trading is as real as it can get, forex courses should offer avenues where the student can practice trading. Some courses have live conference rooms or boards where the trader can learn to trade in real time or, in some cases, in a simulated environment. These experiences should also have a one-on-one feedback and forums for discussion and exchange of information and lessons.

For those who did like to get a good grasp of the market and the rules of the game, there are online sites offering courses and workshops on forex trading. These sites offer courses on risk and money management, trading strategies, technical analysis, market trends and networking. There are also tutorials on the latest softwares and tools being used. There are also online sites that offer lifetime membership and support. Some online schools allow their students to retake the course for updates on the newest trends and strategies.

Innovations

With the advent of the Internet, there is already online forex trading, a system that allows corporations and players in the game to do business virtually. With online forex trading, one can check and monitor the value of the currencies, and even trade directly on the internet. It offers trading of almost 15 currencies, and with the growing number of online traders, it spells more possibilities and more earnings.

Of course, nothing beats the real thing. And a successful forex trader's skill and knowledge is developed with continued experience. A forex trading education may or may benefit you, but it sure can spell a difference. With the forex market's volatile environment and fast-paced transactions, one must be fully-equipped with the appropriate tools, knowledge, skill and disposition. The key here is to know the market. Of course, do not forget to read up on the market, learn how to compare the currency values and generally become a better money manager.

Chapter 11: Essential Tips on how to Learn Forex Trading

Many people who have decided to enter the forex trading should educate themselves first. It is very important to know even the basics of forex trading to gain success, but this is no guarantee, not by a long shot, you need to know more than the basics to even have a fighting chance of succeeding. There are different ways to learn forex trading. You can join online services, enrol in a forex trading school, become an apprentice of a forex trader, or do it alone. However, doing it alone involves a lot of risks especially for beginners.

For novice traders, it is much better to choose the safer ways of learning forex trading. You are going to benefit from experienced instructors who are already trading forex in real times. In this manner, you are being acquainted with the real market conditions. You are given the chance to see the actual processes and decisions which you can later on adopt. Nevertheless, it is your own strategy that will win you up.

There are six simple steps that novice traders can follow to achieve success in the forex markets.

1. Right attitude: The traders who are successful in trading forex takes on the attitude of doing what it takes to achieve success. This stresses that success lies on the person who are trading forex itself. It does not matter if you read forex trading tip sheets or listen to

forex trading guru. It will become invalid if you do not possess the right attitude for success.

You can conduct experiments on your own for two weeks together with other novice traders. They are often called as turtles. Learning forex trading is avoiding the trap of believing that you can actually gain success by following someone else. Just get the right knowledge and develop a strategy of your own.

2. Right method. It should involve long term trends. Keep in mind that the trend on big currencies lasts for months or even for years. It is your responsibility to lock yourself into these trends to make huge profits. It is best suggested to use the breakout methods to catch long-term trends. This method is already proven by leading trading systems. Good software is also recommended for use. It allows the trader to test the trading method that was chosen and later on trade it on real times.

You need to know proper charting and mapping. There is already available software that will aid you regarding market moves. It will allow you to calculate the best times for selling or buying when you are able to read forex market charts.

3. Right discipline: The traders should discipline themselves by strictly following on their developed methods even when losing period's strikes. It could teach them new techniques on how to survive the forex markets even when downfalls strike.

4. Right knowledge: The traders can quickly learn the

breakout method; however, they should also overcome psychological pitfalls involved in forex trading. It is recommended to read motivational books that mainly focus on this matter.

5. Take the risks: The common mistake done by most forex traders is trying to restrict the risks. In the end they may suffer great losses because they are being blocked out in the forex market. The trader's direction is right however the trade does not have enough room for downsides. Always remember that in forex trading risks lays the rewards. There is a difference between rushing in taking risks which are already calculated. It only allows you to wait for the right opportunity.

6. Trading in isolation: The trader should learn this to keep focused. Remember that if you are open to the views and opinions of others, it may discourage you if you find it very different. It does not necessarily mean you follow the opinion agreed upon by many traders, because most often, many traders acquire losses.

Forex market is considered the largest market in the world. It is operational twenty four hours a day, five days a week. Its processes are been carried out in real times without boundaries. The trader's success also depends on the right decision making. Learning forex trading have no barriers and entry points so you need to have better understanding before plunging into business. Although some people suggest that learning forex while trading is the best, but it is always your decision to choose the best way to learn that will suit your needs.

Chapter 12: New Forms of Income Generating Businesses from the Internet: Becoming a Forex Trader

You may know about the internet being one of the tools used by so many people to make some cash through online businesses. The fact that the internet can deliver cash right at your doorstep if you know how, you will definitely want to try and take a piece of the big pie in the internet. However, what kind of online business can ensure you to earn some cash? One way is by becoming a FOREX trader. Although this kind of online business has existed for a few years now, you have to consider that this is one of the new forms of income generating businesses from the internet.

In the past, the FOREX market was closed only to multinational corporations and banks. They are the only ones allowed to trade in this vast and very liquid market.

In FOREX, currency is traded against one another. In order to become successful in FOREX, one must know when to trade specific kinds of currencies and which currency they should trade it against with.

Thanks to the internet, the FOREX market is now open to everyone who has access to the internet. That means that you too can now become a FOREX trader even if you do not have a million dollars or pounds to spare.

In fact, with just a hundred dollars, you can start trading currency in this very large market.

The great thing about the FOREX market is that it's almost always open everyday. This means that you will be able to trade anytime of the day and anytime you want. The trading here is also very large in terms of the amount of money being circulated. In fact, in a single trading day, hundreds of billions of dollars are exchanged.

With this kind of market, you will definitely be able to make some cash and a lot of it if you know how to trade in FOREX. So, just how do you get started trading in the FOREX market assuming that you already know how to trade in it?

Basically, all you need is a computer or a laptop with an active internet connection. Then, you will need to sign up an account with a FOREX broker. Then, you will be provided with FOREX trading software where you will base all your trades from.

The great thing about this is that FOREX brokers will be able to advise you on what trades you should make and when to trade. This is why you have to remember to go with a broker that has a lot of experience in the market. By doing so, you will be able to make sure that you will make some money and minimize the risks of losing money.

These are the things that you have to remember about

the FOREX market. Although this is a huge market, in fact the largest, it does not mean that there are risks involved. In fact, there are some people who lost their life savings in this market because of misinformation and inexperience.

So, even though the FOREX market can make you some cash, there are risks that you should always be wary about. Online FOREX trading is one of the new forms of income generating businesses from the internet today. With this kind of online business, you can be sure that you will earn some cash. Just remember that you do need to know the FOREX market first before you start trading. This will minimize risks of losing money and maximizing your chance of profiting.

Chapter 13: The Importance of a Good Investment Program on Forex Trading

How you ever thought about doing a trade globally? Some people might be a bit hesitant to do such a thing, but the opportunity is just waiting for you out there. You don't actually have to travel outside your country, if that is your concern. With the availability of the Internet, you can actually do forex trading on a global scale even in your own home, at work, and regardless of your location.

The FX market seems complex, especially to new traders, and they find it rather difficult to go about the trade. But nothing is impossible once you have learned the trade. It is a worthwhile venture that you might want to consider even on a tight office schedule.

Being employed in a particular company may not give you all the money that you would need to finance your everyday living. Doing some extra work is often recommended specially in today's times when money is difficult to find. Worry no more; the FX market is not far from your reach.

Identify your goals upon entering the FX market. This is the primary step, so that you will stay focused in your endeavour. Once you have set up a goal, you have to do all it takes to reach that goal, but it should be in a reasonable manner.

In going through forex trading, you will need an investment program, and a good one. Do not settle for anything less because an effective way to succeed in forex trading is a good program.

Most rookies commit the biggest mistake of their lives by availing fake programs. The FX market is a huge industry, and the fact is, many scams and con artists abound the Internet, which actually provides useless materials for beginners. This often leads to frustrations of beginners because they have already failed even before they get to start the actual trade.

Find a legitimate forex investment program. Although it might require a bit of looking around, as well as a bit of your time, once you get what you are looking for, you are in a good start.

You do not have to settle with expensive programs, nor with programs promising easy and quick profits with less the risk. You must be aware that though the FX market offers a lot of opportunities, it is also surrounded with a lot of risks. To become like the pros, you need to learn the forex trading system; and you have to be serious in learning it.

A good program is dynamic. It provides daily advice, manuals, DVD materials, computer disks, and other important forex trading stuffs or resources to transform you into a successful trader. Check if their previous clients are satisfied with their services, and see if the company has built a good reputation in the business.

Professional traders regard forex trading as a science, some thinks it is an art; and to start the real trade, you must undergo a lot of practice. After all, practice makes a perfect trader. Demo accounts are sure-fire ways to learn the different techniques used in the FX market. After you have mastered it, you can proceed to a mini account. Here you can do an actual trade but the risks are minimal. If you think you are quite ready, then get a regular trading account. This is a highly effective step-by-step process because you get to learn a lot of things while you are practicing. Always maintain calmness, and act like the pros. You are about to make big money, one that you probably never imagined in your entire life.

Forex trading is done on a margin. Margin trading allows you to control more money than what is actually in your hands. For you to trade one million US dollars, you should have a security deposit worth ten thousand US dollars. This is a typical example with the rate at 1%.

The FX market spans around the globe, so you can trade twenty-four hours a day. If you choose to do margin trading, the spread rate is much lower compared to futures trading. The requirements are also quite low.

Familiarize yourself with all the in and outs of forex trading. Trading globally poses a lot of risk; you must learn to overcome all these risks in order to earn big profits. Get a good forex trading program.

Chapter 14: A Forex Demo shows you how it Works before you Jump into it for Real

Before airplane pilots actually fly on their own, they usually practice in simulators that re-create what flying will be like without any actual risk. Since currency trading is as dangerous financially as flying is physically, it makes sense that there would be a forex demo available, too.

A forex demo is a smart way for a new investor to start. Reading books and taking online courses can teach you the basics, but the best way to learn anything is to get some hands-on experience. However, with forex, hands-on experience could mean losing your shirt. So a demo gives you real-world training with no actual money being involved.

Usually, the demonstration comes courtesy of a brokerage or other financial Websites. The plan is that once you have tested your skills in the demo, you will get into the real thing and take advantage of the paid services the demo provider has to offer -- forex signals, managed accounts, automated trading, etc. The demo is like a free sample, offered in the hopes that you will enjoy it so much that you buy something, too.

For that reason, you should be highly suspicious of any Web site that wants to charge for a demo. Considering there are literally dozens of sites that offer free demonstrations, there is absolutely no reason that you should pay for it.

When you sign up for a forex demo, you are given a username and password and shown how to use the demo system. Sometimes it involves downloading a piece of software unique to the company; other times it is simply done over the Internet. (Some demos require Macromedia Flash, which most browsers have installed, but which you will need the latest version of.) You determine how much imaginary money you want to start with, and off you go!

Once you are signed in to the forex demo, you do all the things you would do if it were a real-world situation; reading the charts, following the trends, visiting online forums to get other traders' opinions, and making trades. The trades are recorded in the forex demo only and do not go anywhere into the actual market since there is no real money involved. When the market changes, the program determines how much you did have gained or lost based on the decisions you made. You are able to say, "Whew! Good thing this was only for practice!" or "Too bad this was not real!" And once you have gained some expertise using the forex demo, you can move on to the real thing and start making some money for real.

Chapter 15: Simulated Forex Trading uses Simulators as Trader's Guides

There are different reasons why many people are trading in the forex. It includes free demo on real time, leverage of 400:1, or simply getting into the action of trading. However, even if traders performed practices on real time trading by testing its services and strategies, they sometimes fail. The trading demo is not enough unless the trader know what he is doing.

There are different important factors that traders should do in order for them to succeed. Remember, forex trading involves practice, reinforcement, and repetition. This process requires refined strategies and skills. So, traders should incorporate forex simulators to help them save money and never start as a loser.

Compared to forex demo that provides real time functions, forex simulators helps the traders to upload, review, and view historical data any time. It tests the traders understanding if they could recognize trading signals and patterns which can be fast forwarded and rewound. In this manner, the traders can retests their forex trading knowledge and find out what are the things to improve and change to stay in the pace of the forex market conditions.

Forex simulators are very essential to traders because they can be trained for months even within a few days of working. It is because the traders can rewind, pause, or fast forward whatever knowledge they have learned. A five-minute timeframe can be set-up to whatever chosen area. The traders can also get trade snapshots, use the indicators that they like, or keep journal trades to refine strategies.

Forex simulators are compared to PC games. The player has a mission to accomplish and repeating the games so many times can lead to perfection. The forex simulators also works this way, it requires a lot of practice, repetition, and reinforcement to be a good trader.

The traders are more prepared before they try opening a live account on forex trading. Forex simulators are serious tools for traders who wanted to learn how to trade before investing their real money on it.

Keep in mind that there are thousands of forex traders in the forex markets. So, how will the traders invest their money successfully if they do not understand the basics? If forex simulators are clearly defined and practiced then a trader's success is always possible. The first thing that traders should avoid is forex trading pitfalls so that they could really make money out of their investments.

Forex simulators are helpful guides to forex traders so that they could successfully trade forex in the forex markets. It teaches the traders on how to trade in pairs instead of currencies. The traders learn the relationship of one currency from the other and its impacts. Take note, the failure or success of trading forex depends on the right combination of currencies.

The market conditions are also important when trading forex. Forex stimulators help the traders in understanding the basics of forex trading markets to the best of the trader's advantage. It also updates the traders about economic events and news affecting the market conditions. Most novice traders can be shocked by market fluctuation brought about by these phenomena. So, they missed the opportunity to trade because they wait for the market to calm down before trading. Remember, the potential market condition lies in its volatility and not in tranquillity.

Traders also study the advantages of short-term and long-term trading. They can obtain helpful techniques to gain profits by being an ambitious trader. The bid and ask price should be understood well in making profits especially when making either a small or large trades.

Forex stimulators enable the traders to weigh the effects of trading with too much caution. The incremental profit on small scales does not make any difference. Placing stop losses that are too tight can increase the risks of trading failures.

The traders can choose whether to become an independent trader or with an aid of a broker. The risks are clearly explained as well as the outcome of trades. In any way, the traders should analyze it by themselves or seek advice from different reputable sources to prevent committing trade mistakes.

Forex trading simulators can help the traders developed helpful strategies before starting their forex trading business. Simulated forex trading is worth it because it starts with a plan, proper knowledge, and skills to achieve success in trading forex.

Chapter 16: Practicing in the Forex Market

So you want to learn about the Forex market, and trading internationally but you are risking your personal wealth if you jump in before knowing all about how trading takes place. Online, you will find many games and simulations while learning the methods involved in forex market trading. The forex markets include countries from around the world, where all countries involved are using different currencies, and when faced against each other are worth more or less than the original valued currencies that are being traded. The forex markets are used to build wealth in, for governments, banks, and brokers, and for many countries.

To get started in learning about forex trading, you will need to locate the forex trading software, education-learning system you want to use. As you find the games, as they are called, you will enter information about yourself, about what you are interested in learning and then you will download software to your computer. In following the 'game', you will learn how to make and lose money in the forex market. This type of game is going to make you more aware of what happens daily, how the markets open and close, and how different the various countries currencies really are.

You will open an online 'account' using the gaming system. You will then be able to read the news, find and compare markets, and you will be able to make 'fake' trades so you can watch your money build or be eaten away in losses. As you learn the system, using it a few times a week, you are going to be more prepared, more educated and you will be ready to use the forex trades to make money. Of course, you may still need the aid of broker or a company to make your transactions happen but you will better understand the process, what will happen, and what calls you may want to make when you read about the news, the markets, and the currencies in other countries.

The forex market is also referred to as the FX market. If you are interested in joining the millions who are making money in the forex markets, you want to ensure you are dealing with a reputable banker or company involved in forex trading. With the spur of interest in the forex markets, there are many types of companies that are popping out on the Internet appearing to be genuine forex trading companies but in reality, they are not. Forex trading can be completed through a broker, a company that deals in the funds, and from within your own country. For example, the US and the European Union has many regulations and laws regarding forex trading and what companies are permitted to work with the public dealing with international trading and markets.

Chapter 17: Mini Forex Trading: Lesser Stakes, Greater Possibilities

Forex trading is one of the most viable options for someone who's looking at bigger possibilities, bigger profit and greater ease in trading and business. Because of its high liquidity and speedy transactions, forex trading is becoming a popular game among players in the field of business and marketing. While it is traditionally for companies and corporations with big capital and experience in the field, it has also proven itself to be a good venture for a neophyte though what one calls a Mini Forex account or mini forex trading.

Mini Forex Basics

Mini Forex trading is good for people who have just started in the forex market and with not enough funds to open a regular account. It requires a smaller capital compared to regular forex accounts, a minimum of $300. With mini forex trading, you can control a $10,000 currency position.

The key here is leverage. Because of leverage, a trader can trade in a commodity more than the money available in his account. Say with a $250 deposit, one could trade a maximum of 5 mini lots. This kind of leverage is greater than stocks or day trading. Of course, it is recommended to start with a manageable leverage that allows greater flexibility in transactions.

What are the perks of mini forex trading? With just a small stake involved, you get to enjoy free trading platform and benefits that regular forex traders get to enjoy. These would include state-of-the art trading software, charts and resources. With a leverage of 200:1, the trader can trade in a commodity regardless of the amount of money available to him.

Mini forex trading also allows for lesser losses as the contract size is only 1/10th the size of a standard forex account. There is also greater flexibility with regards to customizing trades and minimizing risks. Ideal for those with smaller capital, the trader has a chance of investing in more areas of the market with lesser risk as there is lesser capital to be lost. He need not be hesitant with his transactions as there is lesser capital involved.

With the same freedom enjoyed by regular forex traders, a mini forex trader can trade as many lots as he likes. Although the standard trade size is 10,000 units, you are free to trade as much as 50,000 units or more. In this way, the trader also builds up his confidence in his trading skills at the same time slowly increase his profit and trading position in the market. He gets to manage his money before going for the higher stakes in regular forex trading.

The trader likewise gets to develop a sound trading strategy without getting too emotionally involved in possible losses and profit. For practice, a newbie in forex trading can practice through paper trading. But in the real market, he can start small with mini forex trading. There is lesser capital involved and the practice builds up the trader's trading game plan for future explorations in regular, higher stakes forex trading.

An Example

On a regular account, a 25-pip stop loss is equal to a loss of $250. Since a mini forex account is just 1/10th of the standard forex account, this is amounting to $25 only. If you trade in units of 10,000, the trader is given more flexibility in terms of customizing his trades and lessening the risks of loss.

They say that business is for the risk-taker. But if you are just starting out, it's wise to be cautious and think about your moves. In the world of foreign trading, mini forex accounts provide the wisest and best option especially for a neophyte. It requires lesser capital, lesser emotional investment, and slowly builds up your skills and confidence as a trader. In a way, it is a way to prepare the trader for the higher stakes in the more advanced world of foreign trading.

Chapter 18: Should you Try Forex Arbitrage

It doesn't matter what you are doing, there are always going to be options that are available to you. If you make wise decisions in the options that you choose, you will be able to go through life without too much difficulty. Make some poor decisions, on the other hand, and you can end up in a world of hurt. This is also true whenever you are talking about the Forex market and there certainly are a lot of different options as far as the trading style that you are going to use. One particular trading style that is at times overlooked is known as Forex arbitrage.

Forex arbitrage is basically a way of exploiting a trend that is taking place between two currency pairs within the Forex market. Once you are able to identify one of these trends, it is possible for you to make a considerable amount of money by placing short trades and getting out with the profit in hand. There are a number of individuals who are doing quite well using the Forex arbitrage strategy, and it certainly is possible for you to make money doing so yourself. Caution needs to be taken, however, because exploiting these loopholes that can be found in the trading pairs often closes quickly and you can be left standing on the wrong side of the coin.

The easiest way for you to find out if this system is going to work for you or not is to use one of the online Forex arbitrage calculators that are available. Some of these are available directly online and others can be downloaded to your computer. These calculators are used for speculative purposes only, but it is possible for you to identify where this process might work for you. You can then test it out with a practice trading account before actually placing any money on the market and putting your neck on the line.

Although it certainly is up to you whether you are going to use this type of strategy in your own trading practices or not, I would suggest that you are on the side of caution in this particular regard. It is possible for you to make money using Forex arbitrage but often, it comes at a cost in some way or another. You could use it as part of your trading strategy in order to stay profitable, but make sure that you diversify your efforts as well.

Chapter 19: Forex Research for Success on the Market

Trading on the Forex market is a hobby for some individuals, but for the majority of us it is a way to build up a nest egg for our future. We take the entire process seriously and we certainly want to profit as much as possible from the trades that we are making and in the amount of time that we are able to spend trading. That is why it is often necessary for us to do enormous amounts of Forex research and to compile as much information as possible in order to make sure that we are making wise trades along the way. Here are a few ways for us to do this.

The vast majority of people who trade on the Forex market employ the use of some type of software in order to compile this information for them. Perhaps it is a Forex program which looks at various trading signals and analyzes the data in order to see which way the market is likely to turn in the next day or two. The Forex research that is done through the use of one of these programs is typically reliable, but you also need to keep in mind the volatility of the market whenever you are placing your trades.

A second type of Forex research often takes place for you inside of your trading platform. Since you are using these platforms to access the market and place your trades, it is a convenient place for you to be able to get this information before doing so. Make sure that you look at all of the information that is available within your own forex platform of choice. You might be surprised to find out exactly what they have to offer to you.

Finally, we may spend quite a bit of time doing Forex research by searching the Internet, reading online forums and following blogs of those that we like to emulate. This is also an excellent way for you to do your research for the following week's trading or to build on your knowledge that you are able to make better trades well into the future. It is also an excellent way for you to identify trends that may be taking place and that you can capitalize on. It is certainly a type of research that should be included in any serious trader's day.

Chapter 20: What is Online Forex Trading Broker System? the Question Each Forex Green Horn Should Ask

Some brokers are extremely popular people to their clients, but there are those that are not. Brokers may work for insurance companies, real state, and even companies which provide trading systems. They are important people which many individuals can rely on whenever that would need help of some sort. But a broker system is different.

The Online forex trading broker system has a primary function of providing clients with trading platforms. Trading platforms is known as the place to trade. There are also forex broker systems which provide training and programs which teach clients to invest money and how forex trading is being done.

The trainings provided by these broker systems help many trade investors to minimize risks while maximizing profits. Investors can benefit a lot from these broker systems because they may also be able to receive forex advice, assistance, education, currency analysis, stock, and the future market. Some also provide trading ideas and daily picks from newsletters.

The ultimate goal of almost any forex broker system is to make an investor successful. And this can only be achieved with a system having experienced professional teachers and advisors who are able to give directional market guidance and forex training.

Beginners of the trade should be made aware that forex trading is a high risk investment. The currency market offers a lot of opportunity to earn huge amounts of profits but at the same time coupled with a lot of risks. Currency trading can give you a fortune in minutes, days and hours. But the sad truth is that it can also be lost just at the same time.

Currency speculation is not an easy task, which is why traders should not forget to learn the trade first before making any actual trade. An intensive forex trading course can help you learn all the in and outs of trading. The pros can provide you the needed learning experience before entering the real world of forex.

You can find a comprehensive forex trading course that is of reasonable cost either online or in a traditional class. Look around, or you can ask around for a good trading course available.

Additional services are now provided by many broker systems to draw the attention of prospects and clients. Forex is considered as a sophisticated game, which is why you need a forex broker system.

Get scrolling alerts and news for the typical currency trader. Federal Reserve's decision about the interest rate is also needed by traders, and a broker system is just the perfect place to find it. Professional traders often write newsletters that can be of great use by other forex traders, they will be able to provide information about technical and fundamental analysis. Set up alerts are sometimes provided to give traders certain ideas for them to make more money.

Broker systems are entrusted by many individuals to buy and/or sell on their behalf. Make sure that the broker is registered as an FCM with the CFTC. FCM stands for futures commission merchant; and CFTC is commodity futures trading commission.

First, you would need to have an account before you can set up a broker system. You can find a lot of them online, but make sure that you choose one wisely. You must ask about the fees being charged.

Friends and co-workers are a good source of trusted brokers; ask about the broker's information and the troubles that they encountered, if any.

Online forex broker systems provide different services, but they should particularly be quick in buying or selling and automatic execution. The 'spread' should be clearly identified, whether variable or fixed.

Pay attention to even the littlest thing before signing up for a forex broker system. The margin terms are also of utmost consideration. Ask how margins are calculated and margin requirements.

The broker system should be reliable and its ability as to performance should not be questionable. The trading software used by the trader is quite essential, that is why you should first see all the available options for you. Take advantage of free demos, this would help a lot for you to make a decision.

Check all the policies of the forex broker system. Read especially those in fine print; oftentimes it is the most important part that the investor fails to read.

Chapter 21: The Forex Market uses Margins to Increase your Profits

Forex is a nickname for the foreign exchange, a vast market of trading in which the commodity is money itself. In the forex market, traders are buying and selling foreign currencies; trading dollars for Euros, pounds for yen, and so forth.

Forex is profitable because national currencies fluctuate from day to day based on predictions of the nation's gross domestic product and other factors. As with the stock market, the idea with the forex is to buy low and sell high. Buy a lot of a particular currency when it's weak, then sell it when it becomes stronger.

For example, bad financial news in Great Britain means that forex traders will be selling off their British pounds as fast as possible, as the pound is about to become devalued. Once the pound recovers, those traders will sell it for something else, thus turning a profit.

Though we talk of "buying" and 'selling" pounds, Euros, yen and francs, the transactions performed in the forex are not literal. That is, if you want to buy 100,000 Euros, you do not have to withdraw the equivalent U.S. dollars from your bank account and swap them out for a big stack of Euros. Everything is done on paper only, though the resulting profits and losses are real.

Because the transactions are not done physically, there is room in the forex for what are called 'margins" or "leverage." Put simply, this means you do not have to actually put up the full amount of the position you are taking. Usually the margin is 1%, meaning that when you put $1,000 into it, you are actually getting $100,000. Of course, margins multiply your losses as well as your profits, so you have to be careful.

One of the reasons for allowing a 100:1 margin like this is that the major world currencies in the forex market usually fluctuate less than 1% a day. (In the stock market, a typical stock might fluctuate as much as 10% in one day.) With changes that small, your daily loss or gain on an initial investment of $1,000 would be almost imperceptible, usually less than $10 either way. By multiplying it by 100, the gains and losses in the forex market are more pronounced.

With leverage implemented that way, the basic "lot" for buying and selling currencies is usually 100,000 (which of course only costs 1,000). Most firms that handle day-trading on the forex market do not go any lower than that.

Chapter 22: The Basics of Reading a Forex Quote

The foreign exchange market can be a baffling place for newcomers, and one of the sources of confusion is the forex quote. A forex quote is a small bit of information, yet it's packed with numbers that may not make sense to someone unfamiliar with the forex system. Here is a basic explanation of how it works.

A forex quote consists of a currency pair, Forex deals always involve simultaneously selling one currency and buying another; a bid price and an ask price. For example, one quote might be this:

USD/JPY 118.71/75

The first currency is the base currency, and the other one is the quote currency. The value of the base currency is always 1 -- in this case, 1 U.S. dollar. The number tells you how many of the quote currency (the Japanese yen, in this case) you can buy with $1.

But what kind of number is 118.71/75? It's actually forex shorthand for two numbers: 118.71 and 118.75. The lower number is the bid price, the other is the ask price. The bid price is the price that dealers will buy the base currency for. The ask price is what dealers will sell it for.

So if the above were the current quote, it would mean right now, you could SELL U.S. dollars in exchange for 118.71 yen per dollar. Or, if you preferred, you could BUY U.S. dollars at a rate of 118.75 yen per dollar.

The difference between the bid price and the ask price in a forex quote is called the 'spread," and those tiny units are called "pips." In our example, the spread for USD/JPY was four pips. The spread is usually that small for the most commonly traded currencies, which means anything involving the U.S. dollar, Japanese yen, Great British pound, the euro, Swiss franc or Australian dollar. In fact, thanks to the great competition in the forex trading market, some quotes will have spread of as little as one pip.

Of course, for less commonly traded currencies, the spread can be much greater. And even when the quote delivers a small spread, it adds up when you are trading hundreds of thousands of units. If you were dealing with 100 U.S. dollars, the difference between selling them for 11,871 yen and buying them for 11,875 yen would not be much at all, just four yen. But if it were 100,000 U.S. dollars, suddenly that four-pip spread means a 4,000-yen difference. So the spread in a quote is more important than its smallness would suggest.

Chapter 23: Trying to Forecast Forex Rates is an Acquired Skill

It's not easy to forecast the forex markets, but it's what thousands of forex traders and brokers do every day, with varying degrees of success. Like forecasting the weather, predicting the forex market is sometimes a crapshoot, sometimes a guessing game, and always an adventure.

There are two basic philosophies on how to forecast the forex markets. One is technical analysis; the other is fundamental analysis. We will look at them both.

The technical approach examines past market action and uses that data to predict the future. Previous trends in most areas of life are almost always good indicators of the future; forex is no different. People have not changed much in the decades since the forex market was created. People still buy and sell and react to stimuli in much the same way as they did 50 years ago.

Since forex rates change constantly throughout the day, every day, looking at all the years of past data can be daunting. Smart analysts learned to look at the big picture, to skip the minor details and examine trends over a longer period of time.

Using fundamental analysis to forecast forex markets is a bit more in-depth, but it can also be highly accurate. Basically, fundamental analysis means forecasting the market based on external factors such as political moves, government involvement, social movements, even the weather. Someone good at fundamental analysis might forecast forex drop-offs because he knows a country's government is unstable at the moment, or increases because the country has just elected a popular new leader. Anything that can affect a nation's economy can affect the exchange rates, and that's what a fundamental analyst uses to guess at the forex market's future

Naturally, this means having to know a particular country in-depth, which is hard to do for more than a few countries at a time. (It becomes even more complicated when trying to forecast the euro, since several different countries use that currency.) But having that kind of intricate knowledge makes it much, much easier to forecast forex trends.

Most good traders use a mixture of both processes, technical and fundamental. For example, a trader might see that a country is currently facing a particularly strong hurricane season (fundamental) and know that in the past, strong hurricane seasons have meant a weaker economy for that nation (technical). Thus, he can predict down-turns for that nation with some degree of confidence.

Chapter 24: Online Forex Forums Connect Traders Around the World

Most forex trading is done online, with investors looking at forex charts, considering trends, and making decisions. There is very little interaction, even via the Internet, with other human beings. That is one of the reasons that many traders also spend time in forex forums, chatting with other investors and sharing tips.

There are dozens of forex-related forums and message boards on the Internet. Some are tied to brokerage firms, while others are just freestanding forums on forex-related sites. Since the market is active 24 hours a day, you can usually count on the forums being busy at all hours too.

As mentioned, one of the reasons for visiting forex forums is simply psychological: Humans like to interact with other humans, especially when their day jobs require them to be alone with a computer for hours at a stretch.

Furthermore, there are a lot of emotions involved in trading. It is real money, after all, and often large amounts of it. Online forums give traders a place to discuss the psychological effects of long-term trading, how it can become addictive and nerve-racking, and what impact it has on everyday life. You could think of message boards as being a sort of support group for traders, or the equivalent of the office water cooler.

Forex forums have more practical uses, too, of course. Traders find the tips and strategies offered by their fellow traders to be invaluable. Forums are often rife with people more seasoned and experienced than the average person, which benefits the newcomers. And many experienced traders enjoy visiting the forums because it gives them a chance to share their wisdom with others.

Forex forums are also useful for gauging the general mood of the marketplace. The charts and rates give you the cold, hard facts. But many times making a decision to buy or sell comes from the gut, based not just on the numbers but on how the market FEELS. The forums are a place to see what other traders are thinking right now. Do they feel optimistic or Pessimistic? Are things looking up? Are they discouraged? All of this information can be taken into account when considering a trade.

All forex forums give traders a chance to connect with their colleagues and to learn from one another.

Chapter 25: Forex Trading, what the Hype is all About

Forex trading is all about making big money. Some investors have found it quite easy to make a large amount of money as the forex market changes daily. Forex, is the foreign exchange market. Online and offline you will find references to the forex market as FX as well. Forex trading takes place through a broker or a financial institution often where you are able to purchase other types of stocks, bonds and investments.

When you are thinking about getting involved in the forex markets you should know you are sending money to be invested with other countries. This is done to prop up the investments of people involved in certain types of hedge funds, and in the markets overseas. The forex market could have your money invested in one market one day, and the next day your money is invested in another country. The daily changes are determined by your broker or financial institution. When reading your statements and learning more about your account, you will find that every type of currency has three letters that will represent that currency.

For example, the United States dollars is USD, the Japanese yen is JPY, and the British pound sterling will read as GBP. You will also find that for every transaction on your account listing you will see information that looks like this: JPYzzz/GBPzzz.

This means that you took your Japanese yen money and invested it into something in the British pound market. You will find many transactions from one currency to another if you have money that is scattered throughout the forex markets.

Forex markets trading by investment management firms are the companies you can trust with your money. You want to find a company that has been dealing with forex trading for a very long time, and not someone just new on the block so you get the most for your hard earned money. It is important that you beware of companies that are popping up online and often times from foreign countries that are stating they can get you involved in the forex markets and trading. Read the fine print, and know whom you are dealing with for the best possible protection.

If you are interested in trading on the forex market, you will find limits for investing are different from company to company. Often times you will learn that you need a minimum of $250 or $500 while other companies will need $1000 or $10,000. The company you are dealing with will set limits in how much you need to open an account with their company. The scams that are online will tell you, that you only need a $1 or $5 to open an account, but you need to learn more about that company and where they are doing business before investing any money, this is for your own protection while dealing in forex trading and markets online.

Chapter 26: The Internet and Forex Trading: the Perfect Combination

People go to work everyday to earn money in order to finance all their expenses. Some even stay in the office for extra hours to do overtime, just so they could earn extra money. If you are one of the many people still looking for ways to earn, forex trading is a very good place to start your search.

Forex trading is no longer concentrated in the actual FX market. You can actually do it globally. You might wonder how, well it is quite simple. You are most probably aware that the Internet is widely used nowadays; and many businesses are finding it very useful in almost all areas of their work. And now, you can even trade currencies through the net.

New traders can find the net as a helpful tool in doing their trades online. There are many different forex trading programs available in different websites. All you have to do is to choose one website that would suit your trading needs.

Many forex traders believe that the FX market is the best place to earn money. If you know how the market works and with a little start up capital as investment, you can actually make big profits. And you do not have to worry about your investment's safety. Online forex trading is quite safe, and besides, the fact remains that the FX market cannot be manipulated even by powerful individuals because it is the biggest financial market in the whole world.

It does not matter whether you have an office job, or if you are staying at home. With the Internet, you can actually do the trade at home, in the office, or any time you choose. The FX market is open twenty-four hours each day, and you can take part in the trade six days a week. The opportunities in forex trading are immense.

Almost any business venture requires you to do some marketing, promotion, and/or selling. And not only that, you would need a huge amount of capital. But with forex trading, you will need only a reasonable amount to open an account. As you go through the course of currency trading, you won't be spending a lot of money as well.

The price ranges from three hundred dollars to over two thousand dollars in order to open an account. Instructions are usually provided to help you in doing your trade. You don't have to keep an eye on your computer monitor all the time. You can log off after you have done your trade for the day. And a free to check what happened during the trading day in the FX market. You need to check every now and then though, but you can do it during your free time, or after office hours.

You are allowed to enter buy trades with specified prices. Once the selling price of the currency rises to your desired price, it will be sold automatically for you. Even when you are not watching, you are actually making money.

Having a permanent job is not enough, especially to most people who have a lot of daily expenses. Forex trading allows you to earn extra money, even big money, during your free time.

The system of forex trading is not that difficult to understand. But it would not be a wise move to put your hard earned money in the forex trade without proper knowledge. Practice first; you can take advantage of free trials offered by various websites. This will help you a lot in learning the trade processes and to learn the skills needed in forex trading.

You are free to choose your investment amount. The computer acts like an ATM machine; you don't have any superiors, you are completely responsible for all your actions. So if you want to make money the easiest and fastest way, the FX market is the best place to explore.

Try to educate yourself about the trade, and who knows, you might discover the secret to forex trading and earn thousands of money. The Internet has brought forex trading to everyone, and not all people are aware of this. You are quite lucky to enter the FX market, so take advantage of all the opportunities that will come your way. Learn, and learn even more; that is probably the most effective way to do forex trading. Learn from past mistakes, and make profitable decisions.

Chapter 27: The Different Options you can Avail to Learn Forex Trading

Forex trading, a lot of people may already have heard of it, but not all know what it is all about. One may often think that it is for the 'big' ones, big businesses and organizations. But that is not so, in fact, there are a lot of ordinary individuals who are into forex trading.

Different countries or nations have different currencies. But not all currencies are traded in the FX market. There are seven major currencies traded in the market. Forex trading is the buying and selling of currencies in pair. You can possibly do the trade without a currency pair.

If you are interested in forex trading, you can do it alone, but try to attend a forex class first, or practice as an apprentice. The forex market is volatile, and new traders may find it hard because of the risks that it involves.

The last two options are much better especially if you are new in the FX market. This way, you can benefit a lot from having well-experienced instructors. You are to have a real time experience which you can use later on when you do your trade.

You have to understand the process of forex trading first. Remember that the FX market has no boundaries or barriers. So before jumping into the market, you have to know the right entry points.

Charting and mapping are also important aspects in forex trading. Charting software are readily available, you can secure one so that you can learn about it; as well as learning how to properly map it. Through this, you can see how the market moves. And you can now make good decisions whether to buy or sell a currency, and earn profits in return.

Another important thing to learn is forex trading psychology. You should know how to properly deal with all your losses, of course you can't expect to gain at all times. If for a short period you have made a lot of losses, perhaps it's time to stop just for sometime. Don't be carried away in doing the trade, otherwise you may incur a lot of losses.

New starters who instantly gain a lot of profits may think that they know too much. But it helps to know that it is not the same all throughout. Good profits oftentimes encourage more people to trading so much, without thinking of the risks. Discipline is one trait that you should practice and learn.

Starters, who go through forex trading on their own, without any help, are likely not to succeed in this kind of trade, not unless he or she is 'gifted'. Although they may enjoy a certain amount of profit, time will come when won't be able to keep up with the trade without knowledge of forex trading and its technical aspects.

As a trader, you alone can decide which option is best

for you. Learning forex trading requires dedication, if you can pull it off on your own, good for you. But if you think that you need a little help, you are free to choose from the many forex trading classes offered; or you can be a broker's apprentice. Anyway you choose; you can learn so much about forex trading. And all your learning experiences can be of great importance once you do your actual trade.

There is no substitute to proper learning. It gives you a good grip about the trade, and you can be confident that you are making good decisions. These would reflect a lot from the profits that you are about to gain.

Chapter 28: Tips on Managing Islamic Forex Trading Accounts

Islamic forex accounts are a specific category of forex trading accounts also known as interest free or swap free forex accounts.

Islamic forex trading accounts permit clients of Islamic religion to trade on interest free accounts (SWAP free or Roll Over fee) with no extra charge or penalty for the ability to trade in adherence with Islamic religious principles.

Forex trading also became popular to many Muslims. Like any other traders, they have an option to manage their own accounts or open a managed Islamic forex accounts. Forex accounts that are managed are created for people who do not have the ability in devoting their time on foreign exchange transactions. This is also an option for people who do not have the expertise in dealing with the forex markets. They can hire professionals who are available for managing forex accounts.

Forex account management is a very competitive and serious business. Many investors are allocating some portions of their funds on forex accounts that are managed by professionals. This is very helpful in reducing the risks and mitigating any losses arising from portfolios which include bond market and stock. Remember, the forex transaction is separated from the stock market, which is why the losses and profits are also separated.

Islamic forex trading accounts can enhance the portfolios of the traders in great ways. Keep in mind that Islamic forex trading accounts which are professionally managed regardless of the account or the manager of forex trading you have chosen should provide these things:

1. The Islamic forex trading account is not tied on the operations of stock markets. It should provide better returns than treasury bonds or other money generating instruments in the market.

2. It is very important that professionals who handle your account have expertise. The company should have a good reputation on the forex markets. The foreign trading accounts should be managed by experienced professionals. Take note, most transnational firms and foreign banks are employing the best people who always outperformed others. It does necessarily mean that you hired people who are graduates of Harvard. It only emphasizes that the traders should hire better trained people who can successfully manage their Islamic forex trading accounts.

3. The company or professionals that handle your Islamic forex trading accounts should know how to leverage to gain maximum profits. The manager can book profits both from the rising and falling currency markets. It is recommended that weekly or monthly reports are provided for every forex transactions together with the real time

reports.

4. The Islamic forex trading accounts has liquidity. It should offer the traders easy money withdrawals from investors within specified intervals of time and during emergency cases.

5. The Islamic forex trading accounts which are managed by professionals uses tools on statistical analysis to optimum results and maximum profits. It is because:

a. The professionals know the market on trading forex. They are well educated about the currencies being trade therefore they can also accurately predict the direction of the money in the forex markets. They know the right speculation about the money being sold and bought in pairs. The rise and fall of the currency prices are well predicted so they can sell the currency with higher value and buy the currency with lower value.

b. They have studied your Islamic forex trading accounts picking the forex trading system that will be compatible with it. They can choose the system letting your trades to be automated according to its history, or followed traditional valleys and peaks. This can ensure better execution of the trades preventing market manipulation.

c. The professionals are well trained on dealing with real time forex market trading. Their learning experience can handle whatever market fluctuation and sees it as an opportunity in making huge profits. They are also well acquainted with the things needed in minimizing market losses.

d. They know the margins of every forex trading. So, they can manage your Islamic forex trading account in such a way to avoid trading margins that can accumulate huge amount of money loss.

e. They are experts on using the best forex trading strategy that will help you attain success. These strategies include the right time when to enter or exit in the forex markets. Since forex trading is also open twenty four hours a day, seven days a week, the professionals who are managing your account already know the best times to trade.

Letting your Islamic forex trading accounts be managed by professionals can ensure that it is well taken care of. You can also attend to other activities without worrying about the future outcome of your accounts.

Chapter 29: When it Comes to Smart Investing, all World News is Forex News.

Forex traders know one of the advantages of their field is that the forex market is open 24 hours a day, five and a half days a week. But a 24-hour marketplace means there's forex news coming in constantly, too. With so much information coming from so many markets literally at all hours of the day, it can be hard to keep up with all the news available to you.

But at the same time, an informed trader is a successful trader. To make informed decisions on when to buy and sell currencies, you will have to keep an eye on all the news you can get your hands on. Many Web sites make it relatively easy for you by corralling the forex news into one place, often dividing it into subcategories for easy navigating. Any forex trader, whether new or experienced, should find a news source he likes and check it often.

Many of these forex news sites also offer commentary and analysis, beyond just a simple ticking off of the latest rates. Here you will find experts talking about the issues involved and perhaps offering insights beyond what you would have come up with on your own. Some news sites charge a registration fee for access to all their materials, but it can be worth it in the long run.

Aside from running 24 hours a day, another reason there is constantly a stream of forex news is that so many factors can influence a currency's strength. Natural disasters, government actions and other things, both foreseeable and not foreseeable can cause a nation's currency to go up or down in relative value. An experienced trader will look at all this news and know how to predict what effect it will have.

Often, forex news isn't labelled as such. Any economic news at all can affect the forex market; a sharp-eyed trader is on the lookout constantly for news that might impact his trading. In other words, a good trader will have to be an expert on world affairs, monitoring political, social and other developments in other countries. All of this, combined with the more specific forex news dealing with the details of exchange rates and so forth, gives you the information you need to be successful at currency trading.

Chapter 30: What are Forex Robots?

The Forex market is one of the most volatile markets and yet the most continuous and simultaneous trading in the world. A Forex trader profits from the movement of the different currency worldwide. This market is very speculative and unpredictable. Currency values can change in milliseconds because of different factors. This is where Forex robots come in.

Forex robots enable traders to trade without making emotions rule trading. There would be times when traders exit a trade because of changes, only to find out that the endangered value would come up again. For some traders, keeping your emotions in check and maintaining composure and being rational can be very difficult.

What is a Forex robot?

A Forex robot is a computer program that analyzes the Forex market based on a particular Forex trading system or strategy. The good thing is that these Forex robots are capable of analyzing more than one currency pair. It is programmed to identify a pre-determined point where the robot can place an order or exit a trade. Upon determining a particular trade deal where you would be able to profit, the robot can place or continue with the order without the trader actually being present.

Forex market changes very fast. Political, social and economic changes in a country can change the value of the country's currency. Aside from that, there are other factors that can change the currency value. And it could happen in just a matter or milliseconds. This abrupt change can make timing very difficult for traders. About 95 percent of traders fail to make any profit every day. How can you be part of the successful 5 percent?

Whenever you are doing some Forex trading, timing is crucial. This could either make or break your profit. A Forex robot could help you to improve the timing of your trading. This change could actually help you attain bigger profits in the long run.

The good thing about a Forex robot is that it could monitor all the currencies in the world. It could monitor and determine not just one but more than 20 trading signals. With this capability, it could easily monitor all the currencies and let you know if it has detected a profitable trading opportunity for you.

A Forex robot can even be left in charge. It is ideal for traders who needs time flexibility or have time constraints. Forex robot can do the work and seal the deal for you while you are doing something else or doing some other work. They can even continue trading for you even if you are sleeping or playing golf.

Forex robots are not the same though. If you are looking for a Forex robot, you would have to take account your personal situation or lifestyle, objectives and previous trading experiences. Unfortunately, not all Forex robots have the same profitability. Its quality could sometimes be dependent on the manufacturer of the program. There are some Forex robots which would claim that their profitability would be about 95%, while some would be less than that, or sometimes worse.

So when looking for a Forex robot to help you with your trade, you would have to consider a lot before making a purchase. Aside from that, not all Forex robots can be left to operate on their own. There are some which would require to have manual participation while making the trade. You would have to take account all of this when looking for a Forex robot.

Chapter 31: Newbies Forex Robots

Forex trade is becoming more lucrative and attracting more and more people to start trading. If you are a newcomer in this field, there are lot of things that you would hear from authorities and "so-called experts," like using Forex robots and other automated trading strategy.

There are things that you need to know about Forex trading, as a beginner.

1. Not everybody in the Forex trading wins everyday. This is totally a myth. As a matter of fact, there are about 95 percent of Forex traders who lose their money everyday. Start erasing all your images that Forex trading is uncomplicated and can be done easily. Winning in Forex trading is not only about proper trading tools and equipments. It is also about trading knowledge and mindset.

2. Forex trading is not only about winning. There are also losing periods. It is important to know and understand this fact, since there are some "experts" who would say that there are trading systems that would enable you to have 100% trade wins and zero loss. This is impossible!

If you are a newcomer, is using a Forex robot the best option for you? It can, as long as you would be using it correctly.

There are different reasons why an expert would like to use a Forex robot. It could be because of time constraints, wanting to be more flexible, improving their deals, or keeping their emotions at bay to help them make more transactions. A newcomer or a beginner is a different case.

Forex robot could actually make things easier for a newcomer. Forex trading could be complex and difficult, a software like the expert advisor would help beginners understand the principles about Forex trading and understanding the different strategies and systems.

Expert traders, over time, have developed their own "winning recipe" or their profitable trading strategy. A newcomer cannot compete with that. A Forex robot assists a newcomer in coming up their own winning trading strategy. Beginners would always follow a beginner's curve where they could lose a lot of money while giving different trading methods and strategies a try.

To help the newcomers, these Forex robots can accomplish trades for the beginner. Forex robots can be readily brought from different websites. They are very. You just need to configure it at the beginning and later let it run to autopilot.

Its installation and setup process is also very easy to accomplish. Aside from that, there are also videos and instructions that come with the expert advisor which you can watch to expand your understanding on how the system would work. Aside from that, some Forex robot vendors would offer training kit (for additional fee, sometimes). This would help you get some basic ideas and trading knowledge on how the Forex market works and what to expect from it.

Forex trade success is not just about getting the correct equipment and the right tools. It is about getting a proper mindset and at the same time learning the inner works of trading, not from an automated point of view, but from the manual one.

Forex robots are not limited to be used by beginners only. Even large financial institutions would use automated trading software and program like Forex robots. Just think about it, even if all of traders would be using Forex robots and expert advisors, why are there still traders losing? It is because; it is not just the robots that define success. There are other fields that you need to improve on, like trading mindset and skill, to be able to succeed in Forex trading.

Chapter 32: Forex Robot Myths

Forex market is among the most unpredictable and frequently changing market. Although, this kind of trade is high risk, there are still a lot of people who are venturing into this kind of investment. There are a lot of experts who give advice to every newcomer in Forex trading; it can be about using Forex robots, automated trading, or changing trading strategy. How can we separate the right from the myths?

Let's start with Forex robots. What are the common myths about Forex robots and how can they be corrected?

1. Clever and complicated Forex robots offer the best service

Unfortunately, this is not true. The most simple systems are the ones that may work best. The good thing about simple systems is that they use just simple algorithms and requires fewer elements.

Aside from that, vendors would claim that their programs were designed by brilliant people. Some would claim that their programs would be created by people in NASA or top programmers. What does these people know about trading, anyway?

2. Trading can be improved by scientific and predictive systems

Yes, Forex trading and automated trading systems use mathematical calculations to understand and analyze trading signals and their trends. But, are the mathematical calculations some programs claim are really effective. Some vendors would claim that they use Fibonacci and it could relatively improve trading systems.

These formulas could help you analyze the market, but it could never be used to PREDICT the outcome of a trade. If you can, then there would be numerous people who have gone richer because they won in the Forex market.

3. Forex robots can eliminate loss

There are Forex robots and automated system claiming to have zero losses. Again, if this would be true then a lot of users would already be walking millionaires. But that is not the case. There are about 95 percent of traders who lose their money everyday. So, the remaining 5% are just the successful ones, out of those small percentage, how many are using Forex robots? It is perfectly normal for everybody to encounter a losing period.

4. You can leave your Forex robots to operate on their own

Forex robots claim that you can just turn on your computer and system and let it operate on its own. It can finish deals for you, without you even participating in the process. Any trading system has to be executed in a way where it can be monitored and still follow the trader's trading strategy.

The reality is that you can let you equipment continue on trading, but it does not mean that the more trades that you have the more gains you will get. It still depends on how you would make your robot work for what you want and you strategy, not the other way around.

4. Success in demo accounts is the same for actual trade

Not just because you have proven the effectiveness of the program in a demo account, it could show the same results in the real account. Everything could be risky. This is why it is important to check customer reactions and comments about the products. Most Forex robots website and forum would offer discussions about what are the common problems encountered in real accounts and how it was resolved.

Chapter 33: Its More than one kind of Forex Robots

Generally speaking, Forex trading is dealing with the international market. Forex market deals with all the currency trading the world. Because of its high level of unpredictability, some would refer the Forex market like gambling. Currency values change very fast, that you would need good analysis and at the same time, luck, to be able to land a good transaction.

There are about $3 trillion worth of turnovers every year in the Forex market. More and more traders, newcomers and people are getting interested in sharing the pie. But it is not as simple as that. Tools are necessary to be able to succeed in Forex trade. Forex trading is not also for those who are constantly indecisive and fearful at heart. It takes a lot of decisiveness and courage for you to be able to put your account and investment at risk so that you would be able to gain profit.

This characteristic of the Forex market made some programmers and trading experts to come up with a support system that would enable those who are relatively new in the business to be able to cope with the competition. Thus, the automated Forex trading systems and Forex robots called the expert advisor or EA.

There are two types of Forex trading indicators. These indicators would help you determine if the price is going up or getting down. These indicators would also help you in deciding whether you are entering or exiting a transaction. These indicators are also how kinds of Forex trading robots are called.

1. Velocity/Momentum Robots

These robots analyze the price changes, fluctuations and other movement. Upon analyzing the movement of the price, patterns are defined and organized. These patterns would be grouped together and would be used to understand or as a reference when entering a deal or trade.

The rise and fall of the prices would be displayed and therefore would help in determining a pattern in the movement of the price. This would help the trader understand the factors that trigger price movement and at the same time identify opportunities. These trading robots would help you get oriented with the weak and strong points of different markets.

2. Continuation trading robots

This kind of robots deal with averages. This kind of robot is ideal for Forex markets that show trends. This robot would determine if there are trends the market by monitoring the up and down movement of the currency trading.

Determining and understanding trade by averages would provide flexibility. At the same time, this would allow you to trade outside the technical factors of trading.

These two kinds of robots, operating based on the kinds of trading indicators, show significant impact on improving Forex trading transactions. Although, not all Forex robots can be entirely relied on to finish deals for you. So, you would have to be careful when buying your own robot. At the same time, it is important to remember that Forex robots are meant to support the trader, not to replace them.

Chapter 34: The Secret Behind Forex Robots

Forex robots are making waves. They are believed to have provided numerous benefits to traders who are taking advantage of their support capabilities. Why are Forex robots successful? Forex robots are also known as Expert Advisors or EA. They do live up to their name since they are said to have helped in the $3 trillion market turnover everyday in the Forex market.

As an expert advisor, Forex robots provide advice and information about when to buy, sell and close a deal. The expert advisor interprets and identifies the trading signals that they are able get from analyzing the Forex market.

What do they do?

1. Forex robots provide indicators when a trader would enter or exit a deal. Some traders would like to be notified first before the robot enters a deal and the trader would manually enter the deal or exit from it. But the EA could be programmed so that it could automatically enter a transaction. The trader is also responsible in providing the stricture from where certain trade information and signals would be determined.

2. Aside from entering or exiting a transaction, the Forex robot can also be programmed to perform trade tasks like buying or selling.

3. Forex robots can apply your money management strategy to their program and incorporate it in the trades that they do. Money management is all about determining how much you are willing to buy and sell, or the risk factor involved in trading. Some traders would not include money management and would go for a free strategy. But this could be a costly mistake, so it is better to make sure that the Forex robot already has money management or you could input algorithms in the system to integrate your own management style.

4. Forex robots are also capable of placing, changing and removing stop losses. It could also take orders.

To operate a Forex robot or an EA, you necessarily need a computer, stable internet connection and at least some knowledge on how Forex trading works. You would also have to sign up for an account with a Forex broker; they would be providing a trading program. This trading program would be monitoring the Forex market and enable you to perform trades manually. After setting up an account, you can get the Forex robot from a manufacturer. The EA would be downloaded to your computer and would make trades for you.

But there is a certain difficulty when using a Forex robot. Although they can do the trade for you 24 hours a day and 5 days a week, it is impossible to keep your computer working for that long. So, there are some companies that offer virtual hosting where traders can continue trading while giving their computers and trading robot the needed rest.

These service providers would just require necessary information so that they can host your trading platform. They would be providing you would a username and password to have access to your server. When looking for services like this, it is important to have a demo account first where you can check the service before foregoing into trading real money and account.

But as reiterated by experts, having an automated trading system, in this case the Forex robot, is not an assurance of succeeding in trading and becoming a millionaire. It still relies on your trading skills, knowledge and mindset.

Chapter 35: Creating Profitable Forex Trading Systems in Five Easy Steps

One rule of thumb that every aspiring entrepreneur should remember is that to make huge profits, you should know how to do it by yourself, and not rely on other's efforts. Being independent from other people will help you determine what things are best for your business.

To get huge profits out of your Forex trading career, you need to build your own profitable system, a trading system that will bring you not just hundreds but thousands of dollars worth of Forex revenues. Such trading system is available on the market, but as previously mentioned, you need to be independent, and you need to have your own Forex trading system that will help you achieve your financial goals.

For new traders, it is difficult for them to device their own trading system since they do not have too much knowledge about the Forex market. However, even a neophyte trader can device a trading system that will fit on his personal preference and needs in just five easy steps!

Before we discuss the five easy steps towards a profitable Forex trading system, you need to learn first the three main characteristics of a successful Forex trading system. These are as follows:

1. A successful Forex trading system is simple. There

is no need for a complicated trading system with too many rules. It is a proven truth that simple systems work better than complicated ones, and they have higher chances of success despite the "brutal" characteristic of Forex trading.

2. A successful Forex trading system cuts losses and runs profits. Keep in mind that you need a trading system that gets the huge possible profits and eliminates losses quickly, if not instantly.

3. A successful Forex trading system follows long-term trends. You will never cover your losses if you are just generating small profits. Keep in mind that the Forex market is worth $3 trillion U.S. dollars, thus there is no point in trading in exchange for just small profits if you have the opportunity to make trades for larger revenues. Focus on long-term trends and you will be able to see better results.

Now, here are the five easy steps in building a profitable Forex trading system:

1. As previously mentioned, your trading system must be as simple as possible. Integrate few yet essential rules and an extensive investment management system.

2. Always look for long-term trends (preferably on a weekly basis), then shift to daily charts and to time entry. This will help you analyze market trends efficiently.

3. The ideal way of trading foreign currencies is

through breakout method.

4. Always watch for any break that you will note on your chart, which is commonly confirmed by stochastic crossed with bearish divergence. This will be your great timing tool whether you will enter a certain deal or not.

5. You must integrate effective time management within your system. Time is gold and is one of your precious resources. Design a trading system that is time efficient—where you can maximize the potential of your time resources to generate huge profits.

Get away with complicated systems; it will just ruin your entire Forex trading career. Build a simpler one and see for yourself how profitable it is.

Chapter 36: Types of Automated Forex Trading System

An automated Forex trading system uses a software that would monitor and buy and sell trades for you, all of these while you are doing something else. Traders and investors, especially those who are newcomers in the trading market, find it quite useful and provide them opportunities to get the profit that they want and target.

Using an automated trading system is very efficient since Forex trade very fast, based on different political, economic and social factors. Sine exchange is open 24 hours a day, monitoring is very important. This makes automated Forex trading system valuable in the Forex trade.

An automated trading system can constantly monitor the Forex market. It can also be programmed to set trades and buy or sell; it can stop losses even if the trader is not present.

There are two types of the automated Forex trading system. They are the desktop and web based systems. What are they and how they operate? Let's find out.

1. Desktop- based system

A desktop based system, of course, would require you to use your computer. Internet connection is not necessarily needed to keep it working, though. All

Forex data and charts are saved in the hard drive of your computer. It is necessary for traders using this kind of system to have back-up files. This system is not that popular or preferred among traders. Why?

This kind of system is constantly under security or virus threat. Any kind of this occurrence could trigger your software to lose data, which is why having a back-up is a must. Data and charts could be ruined and cannot be recovered. Other people can also have access to your personal and trading data.

To prevent things like these to happen in your desktop-based system, there are methods that can be done. If you have spare budget, then you can have a computer exclusively just for Forex trading. If you cannot afford it, then you can still do additional safety precautions to safeguard your computer and software.

You can regularly update you back-up file. Make sure to have a password both for your personal and trading data. Having your trading software password protected is also a good idea. Have your anti-virus and trading software updated regularly to make sure that they have the most recent virus and security protection.

2. Web/ Internet based system

With the web-based system, there would be no need to install additional software in your computer to take advantage of the automated Forex trading system. Your Forex account would be taken care of a web-based provider. The server also handles the storing of your data; the provider is also responsible in security and maintenance. For maximum protection, your data is encrypted and at the same time the provider has a back-up copy in case your data is lost.

A good thing about this is that it allows the trader flexibility. An internet-based system allows the trader to do trade anywhere. Although, there are some who say that it is necessary to have a high-speed internet connection to maximize the gains and effectiveness of the system.

Just like anything else, both systems have its advantages and disadvantages. You just have to make sure that the one that you would be using would be suitable for your needs. Aside from that your technical capability and Forex trading style would be factors on choosing the automated Forex trading system you would be using.

Chapter 37: Tips when Choosing the Right Forex Robot

Forex robots are becoming regular members of the Forex market. For some traders, Forex robots are indispensable. Huge opportunities for traders to earn big profits or eventually accumulate huge amounts of opportunities are opening up to traders; there are certain factors like emotions that can affect your trade in a bad way.

Forex robots can put emotions aside and deal without being impartial or being biased when making decisions. Trade decisions are important since the Forex market is so volatile and changes could happen in just a matter of seconds. Quick reaction and decision would pay off, since timing your trade would mean so much for you to be able to increase your profit.

This is the major role for a Forex robot. Forex robots are programmed so that they would be able to enter deals that would be profitable based on the trade signals that the program analyzes. What's great with Forex robots is that they would be able to carry out the strategy without compromising your judgement or setting them aside due to emotional conflicts.

If you are putting your trade career on the hands of a Forex robot, then you would have to understand the different things about it. The profitability of a Forex robot can be based on its quality, and quality can be different mainly because of the manufacturer of the program.

How would you know that you are getting the right Forex robot? Let's check.

1. Your Forex robot has great background about the currency pair you are interested in. Of course, a Forex robot can actually monitor all the currencies in the world. But there would be programs that work best with a particular currency pair.

2. Forex robots sometimes would have a particular size of trade where they would work best. When they have to trade in a bigger size that what they are recommended to do, their performance can sink eventually losing you trade deals and profits. Make sure that you have defined how much your trading size or money you are willing to put into risk in the Forex trading. There are some programs which would work even in different sizes.

3. Forex robots are also available in different levels of automation. If you would like to have a certain level of control on the machine and program, then there are programs which can allow the trader to do some partial manual trading.

4. When looking for Forex robots, always ask about the money-back guarantee. If, for some reason, the program would not technically work, you do not have to worry about buying a new one or wondering about the vendor's return policy.

5. Inquire what kind of features is included with your Forex robot software. There are some programs that are very expensive but when you look at it closely, it does not even have any features that could help you boost your trade. There are programs that you can purchase in a reasonable price and can offer you additional information and tools to improve your trading skills.

A Forex robot is a worthy investment. For it to deliver based on your expectations, then you would have cautious even during the selection stage. You do not just pick up something that was popular; you would need to understand how important it is to make sure that you would get a Forex robot or a program that suits your needs.

Chapter 38: Forex Robot Advantages

We might already have an idea what a Forex robot can do for Forex traders. Forex robot manufacturers would claim that this technology enabled them to gain more profit, but aside from this, what other advantages can a Forex robot give.

It is not unusual for a trader to a lose because of backing out from a deal that they think would end up in losing, only to figure out that this trade would go for the better. Emotions can influence traders and make them indecisive. This psychological factor is actually one of the major problems a Forex robot addresses.

Forex robots can eliminate the factor that human emotions could interfere with a deal. Aside from human emotions, robots could also eliminate user and manual error. Forex robots, deprived of any emotions, would be able to logically and rationally analyze the trading signals and determine if the deal is profitable or not.

A forex robot could maintain constant operation. It could manage and trade your account without you having to do any manual trading on your own. It constant monitoring would help a trader cope and analyze trading charts. Forex robots do not only monitor a determined or particular currency pair, but could almost analyze and monitor all the currencies.

Being able to monitor all of the currencies in the Forex market would help you identify possible trades where you can get more profit. It's monitoring and updates are actually real-time monitoring. Keeping in tabs with the development of the trading market real-time, could give you an edge if you would like to pursue the transaction. There are some automated systems that would only monitor a currency pair, but Forex robots could analyze about 20 trading signals and determine deals of several currency pairs.

Aside from monitoring different currency pairs, you could trade in different markets, in different time zones. But still, it would be based on the market and business hours. But commonly, Forex market operates 24 hours a day weekdays.

It could even be programmed to determine points where you would like to place an order or exit a deal. This characteristic would allow traders to be able to enter trading deals without being present. This means more flexibility. You could do other work while your program would do the trading for you. This is great especially for those who have limited time in trading because of time constraints.

A Forex robot could also trade in real time. It could close on deals and handle transactions in seconds. Manual trading would not be able to do this. But mathematically speaking, robots could be a deal smarter than people. And Forex robots intend to determine the how you can get higher profits and trades in a short period of time given several indicators and factors.

In international trading like Forex trading, the most difficult part could be getting the payments. Sometimes, there are risks of delayed and worse, non-payment. Using a Forex robot would minimize this risk since the purchases will be coordinated with the software.

There are great benefits a trader could reap from using a Forex robot; you just need to make sure that the robot that you would get will work for you. So you have to do some research and look for your best option. This would improve your profitability in the Forex market.

Chapter 39: The Risks of a Forex Robot

Who does not want to have some share with the $3 trillion market turnover that the Forex market gets everyday? If you are one of those newcomers who are learning how to be a part of the Forex trading market and having difficulty to cope with it, you would also receive a lot of talk about getting a Forex trading robot to help you with your trade.

We have hear how good this system is and how a lot of people have gained a lot from using it. But how good is it, really? Could it just be too perfect that we do not want to worry about anything? Contradictory to what most people think, Forex robots would also have downsides.

What are these negative effects?

1. Heavy reliance on your equipment

A Forex robot is there to help you not to completely take over for you. A common mistake made by traders is let automated trading programs do the work for them and never ever put even small manual trading. This can turn into a trading disaster in the long run.

If you rely too much on your equipment, what would you do if your computer crashes or you robot encountered problems? Would this be the end for your trading career? Having sufficient knowledge in doing trade manually could save it, making it really essential if you wanted to succeed in Forex trade.

Another thing is that most traders that use automated trading system would just leave their equipment alone. Automated trading system, specifically, Forex robots have the feature called optimization. This would allow traders to check on previous trades and determine how trades have been won in the past. This would allow your system to improve its program. But, there would be times when the optimization process would be too much. It could keep improving its system until it sees that there are no losses on the data. But this could buy time and can even lose transactions in the end.

2. Believing its magic

There is no such thing as a perfect system. There are some Forex robot systems that say that they have zero losses under their belt. There are experts who say that system like this could actually earn a break-even after 20 years!

So, just the same with the first point, even if there are Forex robots that claim to have as much as 95 to 100 percent gain, relying on them too much and letting them do the trading without the trader getting involved could lead to disaster. But traders would have to dig deeper to understand that, actually, their account could end up dipping as much as 75 to 80 percent. Eventually, this could entirely deplete their account.

3. Alert signs

Some Forex robots would use bad money management strategies, like stop loss could be larger than the target. Others would not have any trading strategy at all! Some would not allow backtest, which is something that traders should be conscious about.

Bottom line is that no automated trading system could make you rich by millions overnight or in weeks. The Forex market is unpredictable and could be exciting. But to succeed in this field, miracle-workers like automated trading system are not the answer. Of course, it could help or provide the necessary support in Forex trading. But still, a good trading mindset and skill could take you to a long way.

Chapter 40: Let your Money Work for you with Automated Forex Trading

In our modern world of luxury and ease, some financial speculators are finding it advantageous to do FOREX trading the easy way; through automated FOREX trading systems.

Automated FOREX trading is exactly what it sounds like. A highly sophisticated and complicated computer program uses mathematical algorithms to determine when to buy and sell currency, and it makes the trades for you. You put an initial investment into the account, and then let the system do all the work for you.

It may sound risky to let a computer program choose when to buy and sell currency, but automated trading can often be safer than doing it yourself. Humans are subject to error, to misreading charts, and to overlooking data. Humans can also let their emotions get in the way of making smart decisions, like the gambler who loses everything because he just cannot tear himself away from the blackjack table.

An automated trading program has none of those flaws. With the software doing it for you, it is as if you were always watching every market, noticing every trend, instantly analyzing all available data, and making the smartest decisions.

There is a cost for this, of course. Most brokers that

offer it require a minimum investment of several thousand dollars or more, and they may charge a fee on top of that.

But the benefits of automated FOREX trading can be great. Whereas manual trading requires an investor to study the market intensely before jumping in to it, automated trading requires no training at all. Learn the very basics of how the market works so you can tell what your automated system is doing for you, and that's it. Sit back and let it make your money work for you.

Automated trading is also useful for companies and other institutions that want to diversify their assets but do not have the time or resources to devote to FOREX trading. If a computer program can do it for you, is no need to have one of your employees handle it, right?

It goes without saying that automated trading systems rely on technical analysis rather than fundamental analysis. That is, the algorithms examine past market performance and general trends and base their trading decisions on that, not on external factors such as politics and environmental concerns, which may affect a nation's currency. Nonetheless, automated trading has proven to be highly effective and accurate for many investors, freeing up their schedules to focus on other things.

Chapter 41: Do you Need to Buy a Forex System?

Any time there is financial speculation involved, whether it is gambling in Vegas or playing the stock market, people want to find a 'system" that ensures success. The forex market is no different in that regard. But is there a forex system that will eliminate risk and guarantee profits for the investor? If you believe there is, we have got a bridge in Brooklyn we did like to sell you, too....

You hear gamblers talk about their 'systems," but who are these gamblers? They are never the high rollers, never the people who actually win a lot. They are people who WANT to win and have convinced themselves they will if they adhere to their 'system."

The same is usually true of forex systems. The Internet is riddled with people selling some system or other. They are always very mysterious; the sites never give any clues about what the system entails, and they are full of people giving breathless testimonials about how easy this system is, and how quickly they learned it, and how rich they are now.

No system can guarantee success. It is impossible. The currency market changes every day, and while experts can use past history and external factors to make educated GUESSES as to how it will perform, they are still guesses. You can still lose your shirt, no matter what forex 'system" you are using.

Are all systems worthless? Not entirely. Some are no more than sound advice and common sense practicalities, probably gleaned from other books and Internet sites. In those cases, it is not that the system is lousy; it is that there is no reason to pay for it when you could get the information it contains for free elsewhere.

You can usually tell that a forex system is suspect simply by the way it is advertised. Websites full of large fonts and exclamation points are a tip-off. So are sites full of grammar and spelling errors, written in an extremely unprofessional, too-casual style. You have to ask yourself: If this system is so foolproof, why haven't the authors made millions with it? Why must they resort to selling a system ABOUT forex instead of engaging in it themselves? Or at the very least, why can't they afford to pay a proof-reader to give their site a once-over? With forex systems, as with everything else in life, remember: If it is too good to be true, it probably is.

Chapter 42: Forge your Forex Trading-Strategy

So you think you have the winning strategy for forex trading. Have you tempered and tested your winning formula yet? What you do not know is that there are things you must take note before fully placing money on your strategy.

These are points tested and tried by those who have come before you. Understand the principles behind them and you may well be on your way to trading success.

Think twice before day trading

So few get to be successful at day trading, most experts firmly believe that it does not work, because the volatility on such a short term varies a lot. You will be better off with a long term trading ventures where chances of profit are dependable.

Fundamental or technical

Are you a fundamental or technical trader? Where does your strategy lay? It is hard to be both; combining the two paths and methodology are at times near impossible and at most difficult. It would be easier to start with a technical aspect of trading in your strategy. Not only would it take into account human psychology, but it will also be easier to work with.

Throw scientific theories away

We all know forex trading needs and objective point of view. Nevertheless, when it comes with your personal strategy, it must fit with your assets, investments and plans. That is why it is difficult to rely on scientific theories alone. If there was truly a successful one, then why isn't everybody a millionaire?

The objective part of the equation should be the trading signals you need to use in determining your next move. Now you see that there is balance in the tempering of your strategy.

Discipline

You work in conjunction with your strategy. Are you discipline in your tasks? Ego might get in the way of a successful and fair trade. What you think towards the market affects the design of your trading plan. Be fair and reasonable and you will profit, being over your head and thinking greedily will get you nowhere but down.

Confidence

Lastly, do you have absolute confidence with your unique plan? Testing and back testing with present parameters is essential to get that confidence. You may even want to start with a small amount first, testing your strategy with as little risk as possible. When it works, resist the urge to change it drastically. Do not over complicate your details.

Hypothetical track records are unreliable.

These kinds of track records are just keeping up and expecting the norm of currency track records. This is simply just too naïve. Playing it safe will not always make you safe. Forex trading is much more difficult than choosing which currency record is safer. In the end, you have to make money right? Not make sure bets and not losing, but end up not gaining anything either.

Is your strategy designed to use stops conservatively? Stops are there to your advantage. Use them. Most people place them immediately after a trade. If you think hesitate a lot, you will end up taking more losses.

Simple and work reasonable

The design of your forex trading strategy should be simple, and requires reasonable amount of input and work from you. Too complex a plan and you might lose sight of your own unique technique. Too much work will take its toll from you, clouding your judgment more.

Chapter 43: Is Forex Scalping for You?

Forex trading takes in all styles, different methods and unique strategies from its diverse number of traders. One mode of earning in the forex market hits a popular and buzzing note- forex scalping.

What exactly is forex scalping and can it work for you?

Forex scalping is simply put, a method of earning profit in day trading by taking small earnings in a regular way. This accumulates to a big amount in the long run. Usually, it is done by day trading. The problem is they do not work. This is considered to be just a big scam by others.

However, why is it so popular?

Because a lot of people are promoting it on the net, promising huge returns with minimal effort required. They support this with impressive track records that appear on their sites. This is the reason why they are so popular: marketing organizations promote their site on search engines, making it look like that a lot of people have already profited from it.

Another reason why it is so popular is the fact that many people motivated by greed and easy profit are naturally attracted to this proposition. Of course, when they join, they lose money. Not only do they lose money when they buy the system, they lose more when they trade with a faulty strategy. That is what creates the buzz.

Why doesn't it work? We can simply explain that prices and rates in day trading are very volatile. There is no assurance that you will profit. It is only made so by the stories of those who want to sell their mock software and plans. These juts simulated and hindsight plans did not really happen and in turn, did not really earn some money.

Scientific theories are just that theories. If they have been proved, then they are no longer theories and hypotheses. Experienced traders have learned not to listen to them. Take a cue and follow suit.

Here are some tips to avoid getting caught into this scam:
1. Trade longer term and forget about day trading. In longer term, the profits are stable. You can also practice short term trading which is different from day trading in terms of time frames. The key is to understand that rates per day are too volatile to rest our investments on them.
2. Know that if it is too easy, then probably it is not true. If scalping works, then nobody would be trying to sell the method, right?
3. Get a full understanding and education of how forex trading works. Simulate first and try mock up trading. Learn and understand how the market works.

Will forex scalping ever phase out in the forex trading market? It probably will not be for a long time. They can repackage the system and presentation to lure other inexperienced, lazy would-be traders. Nevertheless, remember that if you trained properly and understood how the market works, then there is no danger of falling into their trap.

Bottom line is, ditch forex scalping: Forex trading was built on tested principles and unique strategies in predicting the closing rates and watching closely how the market flows. It is not some naïve market where you could bully your way to success with some scientific theory and fancy software platforms, unless you are quite serious with this kind of endeavours. Like any type of trade, it requires dedication, time and effort. If you are able to put all of these things together, then you will reap profits that you have never imagined.

Chapter 44: Forex Alerts are a Handy Way of Staying on Top of the Market

So how do forex traders stay on top of things? Most of them use forex alerts of some kind.

Forex alerts are available from many online forex brokers and other companies. A forex alert is simply a message sent to the user informing him of the latest developments in the forex market, often recommending action of some kind. These alerts can be sent via e-mail or cell phone text message.

The idea behind them is that no one can follow all the markets all the time. Even if you limit yourself to just the 'majors" -- U.S., Eurozone, Great Britain, Australia, Japan and Switzerland that's still 15 currency pairs to keep an eye on. Sometimes things are steady for long periods of time, while other periods are marked by great activity.

The sites that offer forex alerts go about it in one of two ways. Some simply send out alerts every 24 hours, offering the latest info on the forex market. Others send alerts only when something crucial happens. These systems use formulas of their own to determine what constitutes 'something crucial," and they may charge a lot more for their more specific alerts. And of course it is still up to the individual trader to act on or disregard the information send to him in the alerts.

Some brokers include forex alerts as part of their service, while others charge for them. Some are part of a wider alert program that also handles your stocks and bonds. You can tailor the type of alerts you get based on whether you are a conservative or aggressive trader, and how actively you plan to trade.

Serious traders who use forex alerts swear by them. No system is perfect, of course, and a smart trader will always do a little browsing on his own to make sure his latest alert did not miss anything. But alerts are an invaluable way for busy investors to go about their daily lives without having to constantly watch the forex rates.

Chapter 45: Using the Forex Trade Signal to your Advantage

Wouldn't it be nice if you had a way to look into the future and to see what was going to happen over the next few hours, days or weeks? Imagine what you could do if you were able to get this information in advance, both for yourself and for those you care about. Although it may seem like a dream for many people to be able to get this information, the simple fact of the matter is that people are doing it every day on the Forex market. As long as you understand the power of the Forex trade signal, you can have access to this information as well.

The Forex Trade signal is, quite simply, a way for you to determine the direction that the Forex market is going to move in. Although there are certainly many different signals that you can look for, some of the most popular are just ways for you to identify trends that are either just starting or that have been taking place for a considerable amount of time. How can you get this information?

Since there are so many different types of signals that are available, you really need to pick and choose the type that you are going to use in your own personal trading practices. What you can do at that point is to find a way to automate the process and to compile the information into a usable form that will be easy to follow. There are many different Forex trade signal programs that are available to do this. Find one that uses the signals that you would like to use, and you will save yourself a considerable amount of time.

Something that you should be cautious about whenever you are using trading signals on a regular basis is that the Forex market tends to be rather volatile. Although using a Forex Trade signal can certainly help you to make a wise decision, the market can turn quickly as a result of a news item or current event that is taking place. In the Forex market, news such as this travels at faster than the speed of light so make sure that you are positioned in such a way that it will minimize any loss on your part. In doing so, you will make sure that you are around for the long term and will build a solid foundation for yourself in the market.

Chapter 46: How to Read a Forex Chart

The forex chart is among the most basic tools in a forex trader's arsenal. Simply put, it is a graph of a particular currency pair's performance over a given period of time. Reading forex charts is essential to a trader's business, so it's important to know how to read them and understand what they mean.

As I in previous chapters every forex chart will be labelled with a currency pair: EUR/USD, USD/GBP, etc. Remember, all forex trading deals with different countries' currency in relation to each other. The EUR/USD chart, for example, tells you how the euro and the U.S. dollar compare.

Along the bottom of the chart is the timeline 15 minutes, an hour, a day, a week, or some other period. Going up the right-hand side are incremental amounts. For the EUR/USD chart, the amounts might be 1.2531 at the bottom, going up to 1.2561 at the top. And of course the middle of the chart shows what position the EUR/USD pair held at what time.

The forex chart is useful because it shows in graphic terms how a currency pair is doing. You can see at a glance whether a currency is getting stronger or weaker, and you can act accordingly. Choosing the time frame helps you see very minor trends (in a 15-minute period, say) or more long-term ones (over the course of several days, perhaps).

You can find forex charts all over the Internet, on Websites for forex brokers, tutors, and on other forex-related sites. Those are fine for glancing at trends now and then. But to be a serious trader, you need to have access to charts much more readily, without having to go to a Website. That is why trading software gives you forex charts, too (you need to have broadband Internet so you can be "always connected"). Obviously, if you are going to be trading, you need to have convenient access to the very latest charts.

With dozens of world currencies, there are far too many possible currency pairs for anyone to keep track of mentally. Forex charts show at a glance what any currency pair is up to, and good software allows you to save multiple charts as "favourites." Naturally you will want to keep an eye on the charts representing investments you have already made, and it is smart to have a few additional ones saved, too, so you can watch for trends in currencies you have not traded yet. You never know when a lucrative new opportunity is going to be revealed.

Chapter 47: Forex Trading Online

The internet is indeed a gift of today's advanced technology. It has changed the communication industry and now it is being used for different kinds of tasks. It seems that everything is possible through the internet. Before, the only way to trade in the Forex market is to be there physically. But now, you can trade even in your own home or in the office as long as there is an internet connection.

If you think that only the intelligent individuals are involved in forex trading, you are wrong because at present, average individuals can already trade in the market, provided they have adequate capital. The behaviour of different currencies in the forex market can be compared to the movements of regular stock.

The economies of most countries around the globe are fluctuating. Some currencies are highly priced but there are also currencies which have very low values. The Forex market is alive twenty four hours each day and so you can do your transactions at any time of the day and night. If you have an internet connection at home, you can monitor the Forex market trends and other vital info. Don't worry if you are not very familiar with forex trading because you can find loads of information on the internet. Gather all the possible information you can get about forex trading; you must read, comprehend, and learn from the information sources because that is one way to attain success. With the internet in your home or in the office, you can monitor all the real time market information without much difficulty.

Forex trading also have mechanics. For you to understand the trade's mechanics, you will need some helpful tools. Before you invest in the forex market, you have to ensure that you have already developed the right trading skills to prevent possible loses.

There are some forex firms that help new traders in becoming more skilled in forex trading by giving free demos, guidance, and helpful forex news. You can even start investing in the forex market with only $300.

Starters often feel uncomfortable but as days and months pass, you can get the hang of it. With the aid of the internet, it is much easier to learn about the current forex market trends. You can also rely on a good forex broker especially if you are new in Forex trading. Brokers can help you in developing trading strategies or in finding efficient trading systems. Aside from that, a good broker can also help you with fundamental and technical analysis of relevant data.

You too can earn promising rewards if you are willing to assume some risks in forex trading. However, it is vital that you minimize such risks so as not to lose your investment. Make use of all the possible online tools so that you can make educated forex decisions.

What are your needs? You must be able to identify your needs so that you can choose a god trading system or perhaps a reliable broker. Take your time when researching about the latest trading systems offered in the market. Don't forget to check the background of the broker as well.

Forex trading online can be easily carried out and you can expect more profits to roll in once you properly use the tools mentioned earlier. As a trader, you need to be disciplined and you must be very careful with all your trading decisions; being hasty will not get you anywhere.

Chapter 48: How to Succeed in Online Forex Day Trading

Forex trading is the largest known financial market. Day or night, it does not really matter; the trade goes on even as half of the world is asleep. It offers a lot of opportunities for many organizations and individuals to make profit. There are many day traders in the market, and if you think you can do it, why not join the day traders.

Once you decide to start day trading, don't expect to learn everything about it in an instant. You will surely need to learn for some time, and you need to exert a lot of effort. Practice makes perfect, and forex trading requires a lot of it.

Before using real money, you can practice through simulated trading and do a paper trade. Here you can incorporate all your trading techniques and see if they actually work.

Don't be a scared to lose a certain amount of money, because any trade involves a lot of it. But it does not mean that you should not limit your losses, you can make use of stop orders. And most importantly, you should learn from your past losses.

A good trader by day should be disciplined. Make discipline a habit in order to make sound decisions, and act in accord with trading systems/strategies. This way, you can do your trade in a consistent and reliable manner. Certain situations require an individual to make decisions based on their pre-set criteria and parameters.

You should make it a point to habitually follow your trading system/plan; this way you can effectively evaluate the results of your plan. If your expectations are not met, perhaps it is time that you make certain adjustments and fine tuning, so that your plan will still be of good use in the future.

Do not let your emotions rule you, especially when you're making trading decisions. A day trader should always be disciplined, and once you attain your objective, leave the market first. Oftentimes people plunge in deeper because they are influenced by greed and fear.

There are also day traders who are quite reluctant to lose money. For instance your forex goes down, and you are still hoping that after some time it will rise again. And to your surprise, the price goes further down. If only you were not reluctant to lose money, you could have sold it the first time its price went down, and prevent further loss.

A day trader should leave no room for fear and greed to take over; otherwise, this will be the key to your losses.

If you are serious with your day trading, you can also do it at home. You would need hardware and software requirements to put a sufficient platform at home for online trading.

For your hardware requirement, you would need a computer. The monitor should not be less than nineteen inches.

You must have a fast internet connection because day traders need to make fast executions and confirmations of the trade. They also need to receive and deliver quotes, news, and other pertinent market data. A fast internet connection allows you to make your day trading in a timely fashion.

Execution services are available online, and it comes in two types: the internet-based discount brokers and the online systems or the EDAT. The first type varies on how customer orders are executed, reviewed, and confirmed. This causes delay in completing a trade. On the other hand, the EDAT enables the trader to contact specialists directly. This results to a much quicker execution and confirmation of the orders.

Software platforms that are especially designed for day traders are often used by the more serious ones because real time data are usually provided like stock ticker and quotes, market indices and averages, charting, market stories, and price alerts. However, you would need to make monthly payments because this type of software usually charges fees.

Becoming a day trader is easy, but only if you are quite serious with this kind of endeavours. Like any type of trade, it requires dedication, time and effort. If you are able to put all of these things together, then you will reap profits that you have never imagined.

Chapter 49: Forex Technical Indicators Revealed

Some people find Forex trading very difficult. The reason behind this is because they did not spend adequate time in studying the market trends and they did not conduct thorough technical analysis. Forex charts are very important and you need to know how these charts are developed. As you probably know by now, the Forex market is a fast-paced environment and you need to keep up with it if you want to earn good profits. Technical analysis can definitely help you and so can market indicators.

Indicators are quite helpful especially when you are about to make a transaction in the Forex market. Most of the time, these indicators provide you with market's probability behaviour but it can't exactly tell the certainty of currency prices.

Technical indicators are very important in Forex trading. You can combine the indicators to create your very own trading strategy in order to recognize the market trends. As an effective trader, you must be able to identify the current or major trends, the short-trends, and intermediate trends; if you can do this, you will be able to hold a good position in the Forex market where you can earn great profits.

Since the Forex market is changing constantly, you need set a criterion for using the technical indicators. If you want to get the highest probability and accurate predictions, you must be able to combine required indicators. By doing so, you can determine the price behaviours of the currencies you would like to invest on.

Supposing that your judgment is correct, you should still consider other factors in order to gain maximum profits from your trades. If you are having a bad day in the Forex market, take your profits and stop trading for the moment. This is a smart decision because if you stay longer (hoping to regain your lost money), you might lose more of your investment. When the prices of the currencies are moving within a so-called narrow range and is not going anywhere, there is no need to anticipate for a big movement. Find another currency to trade with better profit potentials.

With so many technical indicators to use, you will surely find combinations that will work best for you. Don't be discouraged if ever you encounter some downfalls in Forex trading because that is natural.

When using technical indicators, you must give yourself enough time in doing the analysis and studies. There are so many things to consider and you cannot just do it in minutes. However, make sure that you do not take too long in making your trading decisions because the Forex market will not slow down just to work for you. You are the one who needs to adjust to its fast-paced environment. Keep in mind that there are also lots of traders out there who want to earn profits. You need to keep up with the competition.

The forex market is said to be one of the largest places known to the business people. Trading has become a part of man's life since time immemorial. Needless to say, it is an opportunity that provides better earnings in relation to the released investment. Hence, it is an endeavour which requires you to gain an in-depth knowledge regarding the types of technical indicators that basically prove to be really useful. By combining two or more of them, you increase the probability of obtaining a full knowledge of the steps which you need to take on as you continue with the opportunity of earning a generous profit.

Technical Indicators and their Advantage

Many of the traders are encouraged to make use of the technical indicators. Even more, the pros still trust them. How much more for a beginner like you? They are the mathematical formulas that govern the respective indicators. Studies reveal that they are very accurate too only that they do not really come up with a complete analysis. What these tools can do is to show you the tendencies in the market.

Your mere presence in the forex market suggests that you have a perfect goal and that is to earn money and generate a great deal of profit. You should not forget though that the market is volatile. Meaning, its instability paves way to a number of changes that may occur at any time. Thus, these indicators are the perfect tools that can tell you as to whether it is good enough to buy or sell commodities or securities.

As you opt to utilize the indicators, it is likewise very pertinent to remember that many of the formulas include jotting down the derivatives. This goes to show that the data is not obviously direct. That is why it is often helpful to consult more than one indicator to be able to draw a clearer picture. After all, it will never hurt to check out the accuracy of your conclusion.

Four Basic Classifications of Technical Indicators
Whether you prefer to trade forex, stocks, or other commodities, it pays off to think about obtaining a solid foundation that may serve as your guide. Again, it is very significant to pick out those which you know are already proven to work and those that you can comfortably use.

The trend indicators: Moving averages, Parabolic SAR, and MACD are just some of those that make up this group. By looking into the movement of the trends, you can decide on the level at which you can start trading.

The momentum indicators: These are considered to be the oscillating indicators and are most clear-cut in pinpointing the overbought as well as the oversold positions. Similarly, they show the signals for any new trend. Stochastics, RSI, and CCI are just some of those momentum trend indicators.

The volume indicators: The name itself tells you that the price movement is very much dependent on the volumes of the trades. Generally, the price movement which is rooted from a high volume gathers a fairly stronger signal compared to one which is inspired by the low volume. Examples of which include the force index, money flow index, ease of movement, Chaikin money flow, and many others.

The volatility indicators: They normally look into the ranges that define the volume that lies beneath the movements and the price behaviour. The common examples include the average true range, Bollinger bands, and the envelopes.

There you go with the four groups of technical indicators that will steer you as you work on achieving the best of the profits from the forex market.

Chapter 50: Forex Trading Signals: Indicators of a Better Timing Trade

Forex trading signals that most traders want are selected through shopping for a chart containing useful forex trading indicators. These indicators would work best if a wiser approach is used by the traders to create a trading system that is unique from others.

Forex trading signals provides clearly explained technical indicators to the traders. These signals pertains to price actions which set off either the market entry or market exit, or set off adjustments in any intra-trade types.

A precise mathematical formula being applied to the prices refers to technical indicators. It also displays the intervals of time within the selected periods of prices. So, the charts contain information about technical indicators as well as the prices in the different intervals of time. The data in these charts are always updated depending on its type. Take for instance, a one-minute chart is being updated every after one minute while a sixty-minute chart is updated every after one hour.

If you have understood these intervals and its effects on the technical indicators, then you can start finding the forex trading signals appropriate for you before entering the market.

Potential traders are always looking for easy and clear technical signals. It indicates the right time when a particular trader should enter the market. Remember that forex trading signals are based on a specified chart interval. It is helpful for traders to always observe the chart before entering the market. They can also have an option to use these signals basing from one or more intervals of time to build any entry signal.

If ever you have identified the trade through entry signals, then concentrate next on your exit plans. As a trader, you always have the options of limit exits, exit signals, trailing stops, or fixed stops on the trade.

The trader can also use the forex trading signals when entering a trade to attempt in capturing a reversal. Take for example, if a short swing of a currency pair occurs, you will then capture it earlier as possible because you can accumulate better profit when the swing turns long. This is called the turning points which are excellent signals for market entry and market exits of shorter trades.

Normally, limit exits are preferred by most traders. They are frequently trading using higher percentage, however for only lower pips. Another alternative view that is possible is to use the signals for managing market exits. The signals should be conservative but the exit signals should capture real moves rather than exit limits.

It will be the trader's personal decision on what type of signals he is going to use. The trader should be committed on whatever decision he has made. The technical indicators should be studied well to learn everything about it. It will help you select the best signals which will work best to your advantage.

These signals can be merged. It can also be implemented along with some parameters for improving its performance and reducing the danger of wrong moves. Take note, forex trading signals are characterized as unique market aspects. Using different signal varieties will provide a good system of balances and checks. It enables the traders to anticipate the market movements and conditions before making their trading decision.

Keep in mind that trading forex is difficult especially if it is done only as part-time. It could be easier if you are using your computer twenty four hours each day. Many independent companies and forex brokers have created trading systems which provide forex signals to its users to know when to sell and buy. The trade executions could be very simple. You can just make a phone call or press a button.

Remember, forex trading signals are operating using a mathematical formula. The signals are sent out through phone or email if the parameters are met. If the signals are received, the user will then decide whether to obtain the signals or not.

There are a great number of available service providers on forex trading signals. However, make sure that you carefully read their reviews. In fact, most service provider's signals works, the problem lies on the failure of following the system. Even if you have not decided when it is the right time to sell and buy, you can be sometimes emotional which will later on distract your business" right direction. The traders should follow the systems to succeed.

Chapter 51: Using Forex Signals to Navigate the Currency Market

In forex trading, watching the market for entrance and exit points is the brunt of your work. Traditionally, you monitor the progress of currencies by feed reports. Either by watching the news or guarding the numbers in your laptop.

Here lies the problem- who would want to spend the rest of their day plastered to their laptops? Forex trading seems to be a perfect business ground for everyone. Opportunities are near equal, and you could trade anytime, anywhere provided you have internet access.

The answer to this is to get a service that provides forex signals. Simply put, forex signal services are paid subscription services where they monitor and interpret the market to your liking. You set of specifications of what to watch out for and when to alert you. They send you results by email, or directly to your phone.

Forex signal services are very popular nowadays. You may even refer to it as an indispensable tool for any trader. Brokers even provide their own unique platform that will cater your information requirements. When you sign in with them for an account, they give you this service with a fee or even free.

What usually happens is that they give you signals for known or popular currency pairs. For instance, you may be intent in watching the changes in Euros and American dollars, Japanese Yen and Singaporean dollars. If requested on your account, they can provide you with signals on less known pairs. Whatever your strategy and currency trade is, they can fit their services for your needs.

How do they do this?

Well, forex signal companies use computerized systems to monitor pairs and make some analysis for their subscribers. Understand that they do not make decisions for their subscribers mind you; they are just signals, tools to help you make a decision. Once you make a decision right away, your broker and software can even do the trade right away.

However, there is a catch: they are not a hundred percent accurate. They only provide leanings or advice on what decisions traders should make. The best signal service companies have good track records of providing great recommendations and near accurate signals. The service will cost you, but if you are a serious trader upping their game, then signals are a must.

Here are some tips how to make the most out of your service:

1. Ask about the features from your service provider. If the service comes from your broker, then consider if they are effective for you. Some are packaged into the type of

accounts.

2. List down what are the things you need to monitor. You might save money on services by getting a less costly subscription that just gives what you need.
3. Invest on the reputable forex signal service companies. Their excellent service might be just what you need to gain an edge.

Many brokers and other forex-related businesses offer forex signals to subscribers. Forex signals are simply recommendations to buy or sell based on mathematical algorithms and professional know-how. Usually these signals include specific entry, stop and target levels. They might say something like, in essence, "Right now the EUR/USD bid is at 1.2529 and dropping. When it gets to 1.2465, sell."

Forex signal providers usually charge for their service, sometimes as much as $100 a month. For this the subscriber gets 1-5 signals a day, sent via e-mail, text message or instant messenger. The trader is under no obligation to do anything with the information, of course. They are advisory in nature, and the trader is free to ignore them entirely if he wants to. But most traders generally go along with the advice that comes to them through forex signals. They would not pay for the service if they did not find the advice useful.

There are two schools of thought about forex signals. One says that you are a sucker if you pay for them, with the reasoning that if the people behind them are so good at playing the market, why do they have to sell signals to make a living? The opposing point of view says that since signals require analysis and experience to create, why shouldn't the people who distribute them get paid for their efforts?

If you do choose to pay for a signals service, you should get a trial membership first. Be wary of a service that won't give you a free trial period before you start paying, or that only offers a trial period of a couple days. (What do they have to hide? If their service is good, showing it to you for a week or two will only help sell it to you.)

On the other hand, one maxim usually holds true: You get what you pay for. Sites that offer free forex signals may not be as reliable or experienced as the professional sites. And in either case, you should not blindly follow the advice of forex signals. A smart investor will look at the trends himself to make sure he agrees with the signals he received. The decision to buy or sell is ultimately his, after all.

At the end, what you should remember is that forex signals are just instruments that help you. They are not meant to replace you decision-making process. You alone should decide the trade you have to make. After all, you would not risk all of your money based solely on a machine. You and your strategy must still take control. Forex signals makes forex trading more manageable and more enticing to other people.

Chapter 52: Factors that Influence Forex Market Trends

It is important to be familiar with certain factors that influence trends in the Forex market if you are decided in joining this arena. After all, acquainting yourself with the many scenarios that can cause currencies to go up or down can help you a lot in making decisions for when to buy or sell.

There are basically three major factors that affect the Foreign Exchange –a country's economy, political conditions and market psychology.

Economy

Economic factors are the most basic things that create changes in a country's currency. When such economic conditions as a budget deficit or surplus is present within a country, there will surely be reactions in the market and values will be reflected on currencies. Other conditions may also include inflation trends, and the general economic growth of the country.

The more prosperous a country's economy is the more investors will be able to adhere to doing trade in a more positive attitude. Such indicators as a growth in a nation's gross domestic product (GDP), employment levels and retail sales among others will basically attract more investors and that nation's currency value will likely go up.

Political Conditions

Another very important factor that influence trends in Forex, are the conditions of a country's political sector. This is because political instability or turmoil can generally create negative fluctuations to an economy. But if such instances occur wherein a country may rise above political obstacles, the opposite may occur and the economy may improve.

Events in a region can surely create negative or positive interest among investors for a nation's currency. And so, such conditions surely influence the trends for demands and prices of a certain currency.

Market Psychology

Of course, the perception of traders and investors will greatly influence the Foreign Exchange market in so many ways. After all, the market is highly dependent on whether or not people would want to invest on a country's economy in order to determine whether currency prices will go up or down.

For example, such conditions wherein unsettling international events may happen, then under the "flight of quality" rule, people would generally want to look for a safe haven for their investments. Whenever there is a greater demand for a certain country's economy, then a higher price will be given to buyers and the currency's value will go up and become stronger.

Other events that contribute to traders" perceptions

may be long-term trends where people invest based on what they have seen for a long period and time, and even economic numbers where people may base their investments depending on what numbers show a greater value.

The market in Foreign Exchange is often unpredictable and fluctuating. Therefore if you are interested in doing trades in this market, make sure that you take the time to be knowledgeable about good strategies that can help you play the game.

But more importantly, keep in updating yourself with the different economic trends in the international scene. After all, this currency market would greatly revolve upon events that would occur in the different countries. Familiarizing yourself with the factors that affect the Forex will surely help you make better decisions.

Chapter 53: Hedging Your Bets Against the Future

Aside from signals, you can use another equally useful instrument in forex trading. Options can mean a world of difference when used wisely.

What is an option? Essentially, an option is an agreement or contract that gives power to trade currency at a pre-determined specific price. It is called such because this power is optional- the holder of the contract is not obligated to use it.

In the forex market, there exist two kinds of options:

1.   Call Options

Call options gives the power to buy currency at a specific price. It increases in value when the underlying stock goes up. In a nutshell, what you need to do is to buy call options on a stock when you predict its price is about to go up.

2.   Put Options

Put options, on the other hand, is the power to sell the currency to someone else at a pre-determined price. You buy Put options if in your prediction, the stock of that currency is about to go down.

Here is the point: you buy or sell the stock to make a profit by buying the options and then selling them in turn those options to someone else for a profit.

At the end of the contract, the value of those options will be what is indicated in that contract. Other than that, anytime the value of that option is the value in the current market, where the holder has deemed that he would be making a profit. He has foreseen that his call options would go up and/or his put options will go down.

It may seem complicated at first, but it will all make sense once you get the principle. Remember that call options go up and put options go down.

Now add the concept of leveraging to the idea of options and the possibilities of profit would be staggering. Leveraging is the chance to borrow your broker's assets to trade for currency. So in effect, if you can buy put options at the right time, and sell them at the right time, your profits would greater.

Companies also use options to lower the risk in forex trades. Think of it, you can buy without being bound by the rules of the current fluctuation in the market. It just adds a new dimension to forex trading. Whether the underlying stock moves up or down, there is possibility for profit. Add to that the power of leveraging, and then we can make more profit. This only works if we can correctly call the movements of the currency stocks in mind.

And this is only the tip of the iceberg. The idea gets more complicated as we compute the intrinsic values of the stocks and how companies use options to protect themselves from risks. Nevertheless, the basic principle remains the same: by trading options instead of stock, bigger returns are possible. On the other side, leveraging can also put you in a big risk.

This is why you have to have a sound forex trading strategy first, and you are confident enough to call the movement of the stock values. Once you are ready, then the possibilities of huge profits will all open for you. Learn more about options and the flow of forex trading; they will be your prime weapons to attain market success.

All speculation-based markets are full of uncertainty and none more so than the forex market. A currency might be strong and vibrant today, weak and sickly a month from now. One way to guard against major fluctuations like that is through forex option trading.

A forex option is when you buy the right but not the obligation to buy or sell a particular currency at a particular rate any time between now and the expiration date of the option.

Let's say you are worried that the Japanese yen is going to drop in value sometime in the next six months. You might buy an option that basically locks in the current exchange rate for whatever period of time the option seller allows, usually anywhere from 30 days to six months. You set a number of yen, too. Say you choose 10,000 yen at a rate of 116 yen per U.S. dollar for three months. The option basically says, "I may want to sell 10,000 yen sometime in the next three months, but I am worried the yen is going to devalue in that time. So I have locked in this rate of USD/JPY 116."

Then three months pass. If your prediction was correct and the yen has weakened in that time, say it's now USD/JPY 122 then you exercise your right to sell 10,000 yen at the rate you bought three months earlier. Everyone else selling yen today (everyone who didn't have a forex option, that is) is selling it at 122 per U.S. dollar, and you get to sell it at 116.

If, on the other hand, the yen has stayed the same or gotten stronger, you are under no obligation to actually sell that 10,000 yen your option talked about. You can simply do nothing, and all you have lost is the premium you originally paid for the option.

Ah yes, there is a premium. Brokers who sell forex options charge a fee for the privilege. Think of it as insurance; calling it a "premium" certainly fits. The price of a forex option for 10,000 yen for three months might be $200, which you must pay up front. If the yen drops enough in value, you will hopefully turn enough of a profit to make up for the $200 you had to pay. If it increases in value, and you wind up not exercising the option, all you have lost is the $200 premium.

Forex option trading used to be done only by major banks and corporations, but now many brokers who cater to individual traders offer the service, too. If you are a heavy-duty trader, a forex option is definitely something to consider to guard against future setbacks in the currency you hold.

Chapter 54: Forex Trading: Information that you should Always Watch out For

Getting the necessary and the right information is one of the most important things in order to be successful.

In a company, in the military, in the government, and virtually in any kind of organization, getting the right information is necessary to make the right decision. This is where all decisions are based from. Information plays a vital role in the society.

For example, in the military, making the right decisions during war or even during peacetime is necessary to save and protect lives. In the business world, it is also necessary to get the right information to make the right decision in order for a company to grow and improve net profit.

Most wrong decisions are usually made because of lack of information or because of getting the wrong information.

Here is another example on what happens when decision makers get the wrong information. Countless leaders of countries have been ousted because of one minor glitch in the information that their advisers gave them.

It cannot be stressed enough that it is necessary for

everyone to get the right information. After getting the information, you should study it, and formulate a decision that you think is right for the current situation.

This is also true in the financial market, such as the Forex market.

It is a fact that the Forex market made lots of people rich and also taken a lot of people in the brink of financial collapse. The Forex market can really be a difficult market for you, as an investor. It can only mean two things, either you make it big by getting lots of money or you can really lose big time.

With the constant oscillation of currency value in this market, it is necessary for you, as an investor to obtain the right information to base your decisions from. The right and wrong information or late information can mean the difference of you hitting the jackpot by earning lots of money or you losing a lot of money.

Having the necessary skills and knowledge about the Forex market is simply not enough for an investor to be successful. It is a known fact that there are lots of seasoned Forex investors or traders who have lost a lot of money in this financial market. Some even got into debt or bankruptcy.

This is why you should first consider your options whether you should join the Forex market or not. However, the fact that you can make lots of money in this market can really attract you. Besides, the Forex market can offer you a chance to make the big bucks.

So, if you want to join the Forex market or if you already have an active, funded account, you should make sure that you have access to the right kind of information.

It is recommended that you should hire technical and/or fundamental analysts or brokers if you do not know a thing about Forex charts and graphs. The news also plays an important role in the Forex market.

These people can help you make the right kind of decision by informing you with all the necessary information on what currency you should buy and sell.

Although they will charge you a fee for their services, you can be sure that you will be getting the right information on time that will help you in your decision-making. So, to make it short, you should hire these people's services.

Even if you know how to read the charts, there are simply too many things that you have to consider; there are just simply so many indicators about the different aspects in the Forex market that you should keep an eye on. Simply reading one kind of chart can be very difficult. Try combining it with another chart, and not to mention that you still have to make decisions.

Always remember, if you want to be successful in the

world's largest financial market in the world, you should get informed with the right information on time. You should always keep in mind that the information that analysts and brokers provide you is the key to success.

Chapter 55: Stock Trading and Forex

Today, there are so many forms of trading but two of the most viable for people are the stock trading and the foreign exchange or forex. For you to understand which one would suit your preference best it would be good to understand the difference and similarities between the two before you make that final decision.

In stock trading, the first thing that you need to understand is what "stocks" means. As defined, "stocks" are the "smallest unit of ownership in a company". Here, since you own a share of a company's stock, you are a part owner of the company, thus, you reserve the right to vote on members of the board of directors of the company as well as in other matters concerning the company.

There are actually two types of stock. The "common stock" and the "preferred stock". The first type is the kind that mostly held by the majority of individuals while the other is just like the first type, only that it restricts you to have more freedom than the former except in the "dividends" area.

Forex or Foreign Exchange refers to a market wherein the different currencies in the world are circulated. Simply put, "forex" refers to the market where one can find almost all currencies across the globe and gain profit from it. In forex, all of the global trades are rooted in a real time. Here, the transactions for goods and services are done 24/7 all over the world. These transactions for specific kinds of services and goods are usually done across the national borders, thus, requiring for non-domestic currencies as payments.

Some people often confuse the stock market with the foreign market. This is because they think that they both have the same operations and functions in dealing and transacting business. But, there are big differences between the two. A good trader must know it at heart to be able to deal with the challenges in the forex and came out triumphant in it.

The major difference

Experts say that is very important to understand what sets forex apart from other types of market out there. People who are planning to get into it should familiarize themselves with the structure of the forex to be able to come up with strategies and approaches that will create an impact to the market and will generate a lot of transactions across the globe.

The first thing that sets forex apart from other markets is time or the time frame. Experts say a good trader in the forex should know that this industry is the only industry that literally runs 24 hours a day and 7 days a week. This understanding will lead the trader to come up with various techniques and methods to make transacting easier, efficient and good results.

Another thing that sets forex apart is the absence of exchanges. In the forex, there are no exchanges in terms of transactions but there is what they call the "exchange-based" forex that usually come in the forms of futures.

Where forex transactions are done is what also sets forex apart. Unlike in other markets, the transactions in forex trading are coursed through the inter-bank market wherein the bank itself will directly handle the financial transactions coming from various local and international dealers and brokers.

Over the years, more and more people are fascinated and interested in getting into stock trading and forex this is because they are now seeing how viable and profitable the process could be. But of course, this can only be beneficial to those who understand the market very well.

Chapter 56: The Advantages of Forex Trading in the Stock Markets

Forex is the popular term for foreign exchange markets. The banks and brokerage firms are linked via electronic network to do business in the stock markets. The network allows them to convert currencies worldwide. It became the chief and largest liquefied financial market around the globe. Take for instance, the volume of dollar currencies can rapidly increase in trillions of dollars within a day in currency markets. It even goes beyond the total volume of the total equities in the U.S. as well as future markets.

Forex trading is dominated often by commercial banks, investment banks, and government central banks. This is the main reason why many private investors are dealing on currency exchanges.

They find it easier to access the market through technological innovations such as the internet. It also provides the needed information in the stocks market regarding trading forex. The currencies which are widely traded include British Pound, US Dollar, Japanese Yen, Swiss Franc, Australian Dollar, and Canadian Dollar. Forex trading is done 5 days within a week and the traders can have constant access to various dealers all around the world. The trading does not mainly focus on any exchange or physical location and the transaction happens between two persons via electronic network or a phone line.

Forex trading has grown rapidly on the global market. The restrictions on the flow of capital have even been put off in various countries. This factor leads to market independence settling the forex rates on its perceived values. There are different reasons why forex trading is very popular. It include utmost liquidity, available leverage, lower trading costs.

There are different advantages of forex trading in the stock markets. Traders are making bigger sums of money by selling and buying foreign currencies. However, some people might ask of its advantages on the stock market.

1. Liquidity. Forex market can handle transactions even if it reaches 3 trillion dollars every day. Take note, this is a very large volume. It only denotes that sellers and buyers are always available regardless of the currency types. So, if the trader wanted to buy, there is always an available seller, and if the trader wanted to sell, there is always an available buyer.

2. There is no insider in the trading systems. Remember, constant value fluctuations of several currencies are caused by economic change. Some traders may obtain the information before others get it. So, they can sell or buy it within the stock markets. However, the nation's economy is accessible to every trader so nobody can take an inside advantage to anyone.

3. It has accessibility. It is operational for five days within a week and accessible for twenty four hours. Trading can be made during this period.

4. It has more predictability. It always follow the market trends even the trends that are well established.

5. It can allow smaller investments. The potential traders can open mini accounts even for a few bucks of dollars. Forex trading has high leverage which is around 100:1. It only signifies that your assets can be controlled 100 times over your invested money.

6. It has no commissions. The forex trading brokers can earn money through setting their spreads where they weigh the process between selling and buying currencies.

Forex trading can be one of the best systems in day trading. Since it deals with currency trades, it can have the largest volumes of trading. Although it can be labelled as high risks trading systems, it can bring the traders higher returns within minutes.

However traders should be aware that forex trading needs a thorough research before starting it. Never confine yourself with only one source. Always make it a part of your plan to research first before engaging yourself in the real forex trading. It is not enough to know its advantages. As a trader, you need to clearly understand the systems involved in forex trading.

It is also important to find the best forex trading systems. In this manner, you can incorporate a course, software, or method developed by forex trading experts. Take note, there are various system types that are available. It is important to find the right system that will fit in your goals in the industry of trading forex to achieve success.

Chapter 57: Forex Trading: What to Trade, When to Trade, and how to Trade

Trading in the world's largest and the most liquid financial market is one of the best ways to earn money. Here, if you know how, when, and what to trade, you can be sure that you can earn huge amounts of profit. It is a fact that a lot of people who traded in this financial market became successful and became very rich almost overnight.

As a trader, you would want to grab the opportunity to earn lots of money and of course, start a trading career in Forex.

In the past, because of the high financial requirements, Forex was only limited to large multinational corporations and financial institutions, such as banks. However, because of the advancement of the communications technology and also the existence of high speed internet, Forex in the late 90s is now available for everyone who is interested in trading in the Forex market.

Forex trading, for a beginner trader, is simply the buying and selling of different currencies of the world. This may seem simple enough for everyone, but you should also consider that a lot of inexperienced traders and some experienced traders have suffered huge financial losses in Forex.

You should always keep in mind that aside from the fact that Forex can give you a great money-making potential, Forex also has equal risks. Therefore, before you enter this market and trade, you should first consider a few things in order for you be successful in this money making venture.

First of all, you have to know how to trade currencies. In Forex trading, all you need is a personal computer with an active internet connection, a funded Forex account and a Forex trading system. There are numerous websites that offer Forex trading. In order to start trading, you have to open and fund an account first with your chosen website. After that, you can now start trading in the most liquid market in the world.

You need to have a fast internet connection in order to keep up with the updates and price movements and prevent slippages from happening. Another thing you have to consider is that as much as possible, you should register in a Forex website that offer dummy accounts so that you can practice your skills and strategies in Forex trading.

Now that you know how to trade in the Forex market, the next thing you need to know is what to trade. The Forex market involved different currencies from all over the world. It is also traded in forms of currency pairs. Here are the different currency pairs that you should consider trading in the Forex market:

• EUR/USD • USD/JPY • GBP/USD • USD/CHF • AUD/USD • USD/CAD • NZD/USD •

EUR/GBP • EUR/JPY • GBP/JPY • CHF/JPY • GBP/CHF • EUR/AUD

These are the most commonly traded currency pairs in the Forex market. It is up to you to determine which currency pair you want to trade depending on market conditions. If you do it right, you can be sure that you can earn a substantial amount of income.

The next and last thing you should consider is when you have to trade in the Forex market. Since the Forex market is open 24 hours a day, you can trade whenever you like. And, since it is the most liquid, you can get out whenever you like. It is just a matter of knowing if the market condition is profitable or if it is falling.

Trading begins in Forex at New Zealand next at Australia followed by Asia, in the Middle East, Europe and ends in America. The major markets in Forex are London, Tokyo and New York with trading activities the heaviest when major markets overlap.

Basing from the times, you will see that there will always be someone anywhere in the world who is buying and selling currencies. You will see that when one market closes, another market opens. Trading in the Forex market is 24 hours a day.

Forex market transaction volume is always high during the whole day. However, it peaks the highest when the Asian market, the European market and the US market opens at the same time.

These are the trading hours in the Forex market you have to trade in, in order to get the highest possible trades. This are the hours that are also the most profitable.

Here are the open market times that you can use as reference:
1. New York – 8am to 4pm EST
2. Europe – 2am to 12nn EST
3. Great Britain – 3am to 11am EST
4. Tokyo – 8pm to 4am EST
5. Australia – 7pm to 3am EST

If you look at the schedule and study it, you will see that there are two instances where two of the major markets overlap on trading hours. These are between 2am and 4am EST with Asian and European markets and 8am to 12pm EST with European and North American.

These are the things you should remember when trading in the Forex market. It is not only important that you know how to trade and know some strategies on Forex trading, But, you should also know when is the best time to trade in this very large and very liquid market.

If you follow all these, you can be sure that you can earn a potentially higher profit than on other trading times.

Forex traders are mostly speculators who try to predict which currency is going to increase in value and which currency will decrease in value. Speculators use Forex charts to spot a trend and determine when a particular currency will increase or decrease in value.

Now that you know how to trade in the Forex market, you can now open a funded account and start trading currencies.

Always remember that in all trades done in the financial market, you should also expect to suffer from losses. You should be prepared to deal with it and accept it. This is why you need a substantial amount of money to trade in Forex.

If you want to earn extra cash aside from the cash you earn from your regular job or your business, maybe it is time to you to enter the financial market. One kind of financial market that made a lot of people earn a lot of money is the Forex market.

Every minute in the Forex market counts. One minute you notice a currency is increasing in value, the next you notice that the same kind of currency you noticed a minute ago is decreasing in value. This is why you should consider the fact that Forex market is a very dynamic market with lots of price oscillations.

Minute by minute events are very important in order for you to be successful. Because of this feature that is found in the Forex market, you, as a Forex trader, can enter the market a number of times a day. This will allow you to earn some profits after every number of trades you do and perhaps maybe even lose one if you made the wrong trading decision.

Chapter 58: Forex Trading: How to be Successful

Being a trader in the Forex market has its ups and downs. There are times when you earn lots of profits but there are also times when you lose a great deal too. Foreign Exchange is a complicated, profitable, and risky endeavour. If you are not ready to take some risks, you cannot be an effective and efficient trader.

As you probably know by now, countries have different kinds of currencies. The values of these currencies also vary. In Forex trading, two currencies are being traded which are also called 'trading pairs". When you sell a currency, you are also purchasing another. For example, you can get the British pounds by using US dollars. If there is a small supply of British pounds, you will need to pay more US dollars. In this transaction, the buyer of the British pounds hopes to sell it at a much higher price (more than what he or she paid for it).

Speculators accept the risk of any adverse movements in the exchange rate and in the case of a favourable currency movement; the speculator can earn lots of profits.

You must have your own trading system. This is a must for all traders and beginners in the industry are encouraged to develop their own system. For starters, you can start with a small investment. With the system in place, you can easily decide when to enter the market and when to exit. The cost for every transaction is very minimal and so you can trade for as many times as you like in a day; besides, the Forex market is open round the clock.

It is quite hard to manipulate the Forex market because it is extremely huge. The market is also often influenced by global events and news. Insider trading is definitely eliminated because of these factors.

Never enter the Forex market with limited knowledge. You must be aware that around 90% of all Forex traders suffer great loses. Only 5% are able to gain profitable results while the remaining 5% are only break-even.

You will need to have adequate knowledge about the Forex market. You can start by researching online for useful information about Forex trading.

Try to choose among the many Forex software programs available in the market and you have to ensure that you are using an efficient program. That way, you can easily monitor the activities and changes in the Forex market online. With an internet connection at home and efficient trading software, you can make educated transactions.

You cannot rely on sheer luck if you want to succeed as a trader. You need to study and analyze the market trends while considering market indicators and generators. You can also get a broker to help you out with your trading concerns. You cannot keep afloat in the Forex market without adequate help and knowledge. Know the strategies to use.

Knowing how to trade in Forex is simply just not enough to be successful. In this largest and the most liquid financial market in the world, you need to have more than the knowledge and skills to be successful. You need to know about the different things involved in Forex to earn huge amounts of money.

Simply knowing how to trade Forex and about the major currencies traded, like the US dollar, the Japanese Yen, and others are just the basics. Knowing when to trade and what to trade is equally essential to be successful in Forex.

You need to have a trading strategy. So, what exactly are the trading strategies involved in Forex? There are a number of money making strategies that you can use when trading in the Forex market.

If you use these strategies correctly, you will earn huge amounts of money in a very short time. Firstly, you have to realize that Forex trading is very different from stock trading. Therefore, strategies are also very different.

The first strategy that you can use to earn a lot of money in the Forex market is the leverage Forex trading strategy. In leverage Forex trading strategy, it allows you, as an investor in the Forex market, to borrow money to increase your earning potential.

With this strategy, you can easily turn your money to

1:100 ratio. However, the risk involved can be great. This is why there are stop loss orders you can use to minimize the risk and also to minimize the loss. The leverage Forex trading strategy is one of the most commonly used strategy by Forex traders to maximize profits.

In the stop loss order strategy, the Forex trader creates a predetermined point in the trade where the investor will not trade. As mentioned before, you can use this strategy to minimize risk and minimize loss. However, this strategy can also backfire to you, as the Forex trader. This is because you may run the risk of stopping your trades when the value of the currency goes higher than expected.

It is up to you to decide if you will be using this strategy or not.

These are some of the strategies you can use when trading in the Forex market.

Forex trading is a 24 hour market where you can trade anytime and anywhere you are. If you think that the Forex market conditions are good at a specific time, then you can trade at that specific time.

Also, the Forex market is the most liquid market in the world. This means that you can enter or exit the market anytime you wish to. This is to minimize the risk and there is also no daily trading limit.

Here are other tips that you should remember in order to earn money in the Forex market and be good in doing so:

1. The first and the last ticks are usually the most expensive. So, for most traders, the rule of thumb is getting in late and get out early.

2. When you are losing, you want to minimize the risk of losing more money. So, don't add money when you are losing.

3. Select trades that move along with the trend. This can minimize the risk of losing money and maximize your chances of profits.

There are quite a few tools you can use when trading in the Forex market. One is the Forex charts. For the speculator, the chart is the most important tool that you can use to determine market trends and accurately predict the future value of the currency. Although it is not actually 100% accurate, you can use the Forex charts as a guide to what is happening in the market.

You need to know how to read the different charts involved in the Forex market. There are daily charts, hourly charts, 15 minute charts and even 5 minute charts to get you closer to the action. You can compare each of the data in the chart to spot market trends and at the same time, spot potential money making trends.

This can also help you minimize the risk when trading in Forex. Learn how to read charts effectively and you will be well on your way to become successful in the Forex market.

These are some the strategies and tips that you should

keep in mind in order to minimize the risks in Forex trading and maximize your earning potential. Depending on your skills and how you apply your strategies, you can really make a lot of money in the Forex market. However, to be a truly successful Forex trader, you need to accept the fact that you will sometimes lose money. Never get discouraged when you do. Analyze where you made your mistake, think of a solution to get back what you lost and continue trading.

Chapter 59: Forex Brokers: Assisting you with your Trading Needs

If you traded in the Forex market before or if you are still trading now, you may have heard the term Forex broker a lot of times. However, as an individual trader, you may want to know what is a Forex broker and what they do.

Forex brokers are individuals or companies that assist individual traders and companies when they are trading in the Forex market. These individuals can really give you that extra edge you need in order to be successful in the Forex market. Although they will be trading your funded account, all the decisions are still yours to make if you want to.

Forex brokers are there to assist you with your trading needs in exchange for a small commission from what you earn. Here are some of the services that a Forex broker can give you:

1. A Forex broker can give you advice regarding on real time quotes.
2. A Forex broker can also give you advice on what to buy or sell by basing it on news feeds.
3. A Forex broker can trade your funded account basing solely on his or her decision if you want them to.
4. A Forex broker can also provide you with software data to help you with your trading decisions.

Searching for a good Forex broker can prove to be a very tedious task. Since there are a lot of advertising in the internet about Forex brokers, Forex traders get confused on which Forex broker they should hire. With all the Forex brokers out there that offers great Forex trading income and quotations, you will find it hard to choose a good and reputable Forex broker.

With a little research, you can find the right Forex broker who can be trusted. If you lack referrals for Forex brokers, you can try and do a little research of your own. The first thing you need to find out about a particular Forex broker with the amount of clients they serve. The more clients they serve the more chances that these brokers are trusted. You should also know the amount of trades these brokers are conducting.

Knowing the broker's experience in the Forex market is also a great way to determine if he or she is the right broker to hire. Experienced Forex brokers will increase your chances of earning money from the Forex market.

If you have questions or complaints, you should call or email the company and ask questions regarding their trading system. You should never be uncomfortable doing this. Besides, they will be the one who will manage your money. And, it is your right to know about what they are doing with your money.

When choosing a Forex broker, you should also consider their trading options. You should also know that Forex brokers are different from what they can offer you. They differ in platforms, spreads, or leverage. You have to know which of the trading options is very important to you in order to be comfortable when you trade in the Forex market.

Most online Forex brokers offer potential clients with a demo account. This will allow you to try out their trading platform without actually risking money. You should look for a demo platform that works just like the real thing and you should also determine if you are comfortable with the trading platform.

Look for the features you want in a trading platform in order for you to know what to expect if you trade with them. If you are comfortable with a trading platform, you should consider trading with them, and if you are not, scratch them off your list. This is a great way to test their trading platform and not risk your money.

If a Forex broker is not willing to share financial information about their company, you should not trade with them because they are reluctant to share company information. They should answer your questions regarding on how they manage their client's money and how they trade that money.

Always remember that if you see an offer that is too good to be true by Forex traders, it probably is too good to be true. The Forex market is a very risky place to trade and Forex brokers must tell you that there are certain risks involved when trading in the Forex market. Avoid hiring a Forex broker who says that trading in Forex is easy and a very good money making market with very low risks.

These are the things you should consider when you look for a Forex broker. If you find that right broker, you can be sure that you can really earn money.

Chapter 60: Finding a Forex Broker in a Crowded Marketplace

So you want to get involved in the foreign exchange market, or forex. You are itching to trade one currency for another and make some profit. But you can't just barge into Citigroup or any of the big banks start throwing Euros and yen around. To participate, you need a forex broker.

There are dozens of brokers, who service traders. It is done almost exclusively online, and in fact ordinary citizens rarely got involved with forex trading at all until the computer boom of the 1980s, and then exponentially more with the advent of the Internet in the 1990s. Since then, forex brokers have proliferated.

As you might expect, levels of reliability and competence vary from one broker to another. The Internet is rife with unsavoury types seeking to take advantage of suckers, so you would do well to investigate thoroughly any broker you are planning to use. Does their Website look professional and reassuring, or is it riddled with dead links and spelling errors? Google the broker to see if they have been mentioned in news articles. Ask about their track record. And above all, avoid anyone who promises things that sound too good to be true, or who downplay the financial risk involved in forex trading.

Look for a broker that seems to genuinely want your

business. Does the firm have customer service representatives available? Is there a phone number you can call to speak to a live person? The Website should explain things clearly. If the site is full of language that seems designed to go over your head, look for a different broker.

If you set up an account with an online forex broker, it will work like this. First, you must apply for an account, which most brokers allow you to do online. This is to verify your identity and the validity of your bank accounts and financial records. Some brokers also require you to download their forex trading software, while others let you use whatever software you prefer. You will also have to transfer a minimum deposit to your account with your new broker. The minimum can be anywhere from $100 to $2,500.

Ideally, the broker you choose should offer service and support when you need it but should mostly simply stay out of the way and let you conduct your business. If you can find a forex broker who is professional and helpful, your experience in the forex market should be full of smooth sailing.

Forex brokers are a dime a dozen. What really set them apart from one another are the services and information unique to each one. How to distinguish a good one from a bad company? What are the major factors that come into play?

What you should consider in choosing one for you all depends on your trading strategy, and a number of factors.

These seven points will help you narrow down that perfect fit of a broker that will help in your fare in foreign exchange trading:

1. Types of Account: Many forex brokers offer different types of accounts depending on the amount of capital you will put in. This is important to know especially if you are a novice or a conservative trader. What you need to do here is to research what kinds of accounts your target forex brokers have and what options each account will bring you.

2. Demo Accounts: Some brokers offer demo accounts or accounts where you are allowed to trade by trial so that losses and gains will not reflect in your investment. This is useful for trading beginners so that they can get used to the conditions of the trade.

3. Leverage: In a nutshell, leverage financing is the opportunity to borrow that broker's money to make a profit if there is a chance. Your small investment may multiply into bigger gains, but there is also of course, the risk of losing money. Different broker firms have different leveraging practices, so information on what they could offer would be useful for you.

4. Software and Platform: The more elite brokers offer up the more sophisticated technology to their clients. The platforms where you monitor your numbers, get quotes and compare charts are essential in modern day trading. You have to know whether the broker you are eyeing on can deliver the same features and more. Most traders consider

these useful platforms an essential in the business.

5. Spread: Spread varies from account types and brokers. A lower spread instinctively means a higher profit for the investor. This is where your profit would come from so it is logical to research about what types of spread, whether fixed or variable is featured by the broker.

6. Fees: Fees like rollover fees for held positions are pretty much standard for most forex brokers. There are also many fees that you do not know about. The good news is that some brokers cancel these fees away on special accounts if requested.

7. Support: When there is a feature in the software you cannot access or a flaw in the platform you must fix, a forex broker's technical support may just win your loyalty as a client. Assistance in whatever you need, whether it is software, hardware or even sound advice is a prime asset of a good broker company. It is what keeps the clients in.

Of course, there are lots of other minor considerations and features that distinguish one forex broker from the next. These seven points will give you a basis, while your trading strategy and specific needs will dictate the rest. Research and scrutiny will point you to the right decision of who gets to handle your investment and gets your loyalty in the long run. Forex trading is a working partnership with your forex broker, and a long-lasting relationship can only benefit both sides.

Chapter 61: How to Find Available Forex Jobs

Even though we are living in a time whenever it seems that jobs are difficult to come by, that does not necessarily mean that it is impossible to find the one that you are looking for. Good examples of this are some of the Forex jobs that are currently available, especially for people who are highly qualified in this field. Here is a brief overview of some of the current employment opportunities that are opening up, some of which you may be able to work into if you have the qualifications.

Although there certainly are multiple places for you to find Forex jobs available, one of the easiest ways for you to do so is to go right to the trading source. Working for a broker or for an online trading platform is one of the easiest ways for you to find employment within the currency trading field. It might be necessary for you to relocate in order to be involved with one of these Forex platforms, but there are also times whenever telecommuting is an option.

One of the most common types of Forex jobs has to do with bilingual sales. If you are able to speak multiple languages, it is often possible for you to get work in this field, especially if you understand forex in general. Many of the online trading platforms are opening up to additional languages which are also opening up additional opportunities for employment. You can look at almost any of the growing Forex platforms that are on the Internet and you will find job openings in this area.

Another type of Forex jobs that are available include system analysis and web development. These are also jobs that are typically available within any Forex platform, provided you have the set of skills necessary in order for you to accomplish it. It is not always necessary for you to understand the process of trading on the Forex market in order to land one of these jobs, but it certainly can help you and make your resume a little more appealing.

As the market continues to tighten up and more people are looking for gainful employment, Forex jobs will also become more difficult to come by. Provided you have the set of skills necessary which helps you to understand what is going on within the market, it is easier for you to find employment within one of these Forex platforms.

Chapter 62: Conclusion

Being a forex trader is not for the faint of heart. The foreign exchange market is a fast-paced world that operates 24 hours a day, 5 and half days a week. For some traders, fortunes are made and lost very quickly. Yet for someone with the right know-how and enough motivation and drive, forex trading can be rewarding both personally and financially.

How many people make their living as forex traders? It is hard to say for sure, but we know the number is smaller than the number of stock traders. Most forex traders are actually international banks and other huge corporations; private citizens comprise only about 2 percent of the entire forex market.

Nonetheless, they are out there, and the number is growing. As the Internet and other technological advancements make it more accessible, the forex market becomes more manageable and more average citizens become traders. To begin with, most of these 'day traders" keep their regular jobs and do forex as a side project. It is notoriously difficult to make a living as a forex trader at the start, and most new investors find they must allow for the learning curve before they are really ready to do it full-time.

Once a new trader gets the hang of it, buying and selling currencies with some degree of confidence and turning a profit, he may find that he can quit his day job and focus on trading full-time. There is certainly enough activity to fill a forex trader's day, with news that could affect currency rates coming in almost constantly. A smart trader watches this information continually, almost obsessively, always on the watch for a sign that the time is right to buy or sell.

With home computers and high-speed Internet service available nearly everywhere, being a trader from home has become feasible. Some traders eventually become brokers, but the excitement and the potential profit lies in working for yourself. With a stock market, a bad day could mean disaster. But with the forex market, a bad day for one nation's economy hardly matters, since there are still a dozen stronger, viable currencies to be traded. In that way, some consider being a forex trader slightly more stable than being a stock broker. Either way, there is always risk when money and speculation are involved, but with dedication and resourcefulness, you can make a handsome living as a forex trader.

Good Luck!

www.ingramcontent.com/pod-product-compliance
Lightning Source LLC
Chambersburg PA
CBHW071756200526
45167CB00017B/281